ESSENTIAL MADEIRA

 Best places to see 34–55

 Featured sight

 Funchal 81–118

Western Madeira 119–136

Central Madeira 137–154

Eastern Madeira 155–174

 Porto Santo 175–186

Original text by Christopher Catling

Updated by Terry Marsh

© AA Media Limited 2009
First published 2007
Revised 2009

Series Editor Karen Kemp
Series Designer Sharon Rudd
Cartographic Editor Anna Thompson

ISBN: 978-0-7495-6127-7

Published by AA Publishing, a trading name of AA Media Limited, whose registered office is Fanum House, Basing View, Basingstoke, Hampshire RG21 4EA. Registered number 06112600.

A CIP catalogue record for this book is available from the British Library

Colour separation: MRM Graphics Ltd
Printed and bound in Italy by Printer Trento S.r.l.

A03804
Maps in this title produced from mapping © KOMPASS GmbH, A-6063 Rum, Innsbruck

About this book

This book is divided into five sections.

The essence of Madeira pages 6–19
Introduction; Features; Food and drink;
Short break including the 10 Essentials

Planning pages 20–33
Before you go; Getting there; Getting
around; Being there

Best places to see pages 34–55
The unmissable highlights of any visit
to Madeira

Best things to do pages 56–77
Great places to have lunch; places to
take the children; good viewpoints; top
activities; best souvenirs and shopping
and more

Exploring pages 78–186
The best places to visit in Madeira,
organized by area

Maps
All map references are to the maps on
the covers. For example, Calheta has the
reference ✚ 3F – indicating the grid
square in which it is to be found

Admission prices
€ inexpensive (under €10)
€€ moderate (€10–€20)
€€€ expensive (over €20)

Hotel prices
Price are per room per night:
€ budget (under €70);
€€ moderate (€70–€120);
€€€ expensive to luxury (over €120)

Restaurant prices
Price for a three-course meal per person
without drinks:
€ budget (under €17);
€€ moderate (€17–€30);
€€€ expensive (over €30)

Contents

BEST THINGS TO DO

56 – 77

EXPLORING...

78 – 186

The essence of...

Landscape and climate combine on Madeira to create an island of all-year-round appeal. In winter, while northern Europe shivers, southerly Madeira is basking in balmy sunshine. In summer, while searing heat turns much of southern Europe arid, the island remains a green semitropical paradise, the air heavy with the scent of flowers. To travel around Madeira is to encounter breathtaking views at every turn, whether sheer rock cliffs battered by Atlantic waves, burnt volcanic rocks lit gold by the setting sun, or valleys carved into tiny fields, forming a patchwork of stepped terraces.

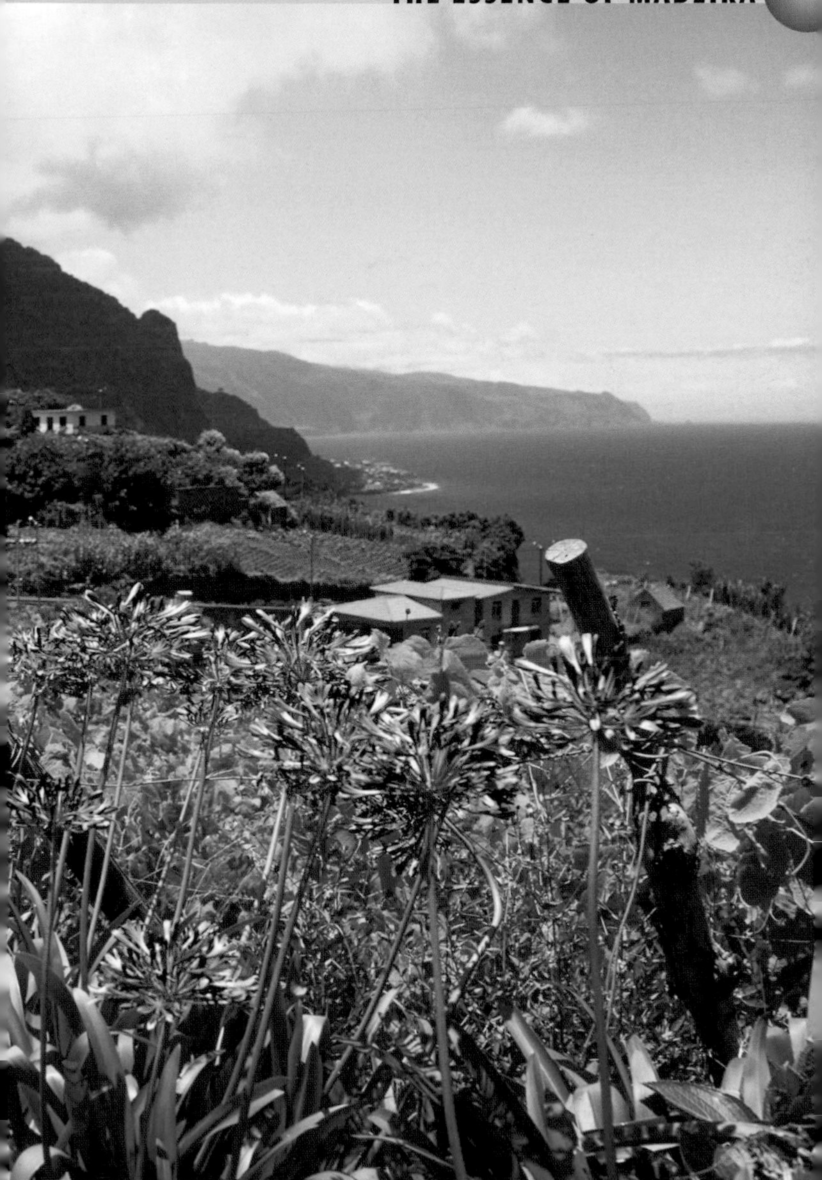

THE ESSENCE OF MADEIRA

features

With its mild and balmy climate, its flowers and its terraced hillsides, Madeira reminds some visitors of Bali or the Philippines. Others find Funchal, the island capital, reminiscent of towns in Brazil, Venezuela or Colombia, with its colonial-style town houses and elegant balconies dripping with flowers.

GEOGRAPHY

● Set in the eastern Atlantic, the island of Madeira lies roughly 1,000km (620 miles) from Lisbon and 600km (375 miles) from Morocco, the nearest mainland.

● Madeira measures 54km by 23km (33 miles by 14 miles), and has a population of 240,000.

● Madeira's nearest neighbour is the island of Porto Santo (population 4,400), which lies 37km (23 miles) to the northeast. The island is blessed with a magnificent 11km (7-mile) sweep of sandy beach.

● Also part of the Madeiran archipelago are two groups of uninhabited islands: the three Ilhas Desertas (Desert Isles), which are situated 16km (10 miles) to the southeast of Madeira, and the Ilhas Selvagens (Savage Isles), which lie 216km (134 miles) to the south.

10

LANDSCAPE

● Madeira is the product of volcanic eruptions that began some 5 million years ago. Volcanic peaks are a major feature of the island, several of them rising to more than 1,800m (5,900ft).

● Christopher Columbus described Madeira to Queen Isabella of Spain by crumpling up a piece of paper: apart from the southern coastal plain, the mountainous island is carved into a myriad valleys and ravines.

● Driving distances are greatly magnified by the steep terrain, necessitating slow progress along the tortuous zig-zagging roads – drive with caution.

CLIMATE

● Madeira's climate is sub-tropical: the southerly latitude ensures warm, frost-free winters and cooling Atlantic winds take the edge off the intense heat of summer.

● Atlantic fronts drop rain on the north side of the island, while the south side remains dry and sunny for much of the year.

LEVADAS

On Madeira you can escape quickly and easily from the bustle of modern life by walking alongside the island's extensive network of irrigation canals. Called *levadas*, these watercourses link village to village and emanate from deep in the mountainous heart of the island. *Levadas* follow the island's contours, falling with an almost imperceptible gradient, so it is possible to walk for miles on level paths, enjoying Madeira's exhilarating landscapes with none of the physical effort normally associated with mountain climbing.

food & drink

Madeiran cooking is deliciously simple: fish and meat grilled over a charcoal fire and flavoured with garlic and herbs. Eaten with warm bread, straight from the oven, this is food to be savoured in the flower-scented air of a Madeiran evening.

Madeira's specialities are *espada* and *espetada*, two totally different dishes with confusingly similar names. Fish-lovers should opt for *espada*, the grilled or fried meat of the scabbard fish, ugly black-skinned creatures with large eyes and razor-sharp teeth that are sold in every Madeiran fish market. The tasty bone-free fish with firm white flesh is usually marinated in lemon juice or vinegar before cooking, and may be served with grilled bananas.

Upmarket restaurants also *flambé* the fish in Madeira wine and add imported seafood, such as shrimps and mussels, to the sauce.

Fish is an everyday dish on Madeira. On special occasions, Madeirans eat kebabs – called *espetada* – made from cubes of prime beef, rubbed in sea salt and minced garlic and skewered on a fresh bay

twig. To enjoy this dish at its most authentic, you have to eat it at a village festival, or find a restaurant that grills the meat over a wood fire for extra fragrance. Beef features again in the popular lunchtime staple of *prego no prato*, a sandwich made from robust country bread liberally spread with garlic butter and enclosing a tender chunk of grilled steak.

SEAFOOD AND SOUPS

Many restaurants on Madeira specialize in seafood, though much is imported and a seafood platter can be expensive. Fish soup *(caldeirada)* is, by contrast, delicious and cheap, being based on stock made from the heads and bones of locally caught fish, such as sea-bream, black-tail, barracuda and tuna. Also popular is *arroz de marisco* – seafood rice – made from saffron rice, squid, prawns and clams. Soups, influenced by mainland Portuguese cuisine, are substantial dishes – more hearty casserole than appetiser. Try *caldo verde*, made from finely shredded cabbage, potatoes, garlic and spicy *chouriço* sausages, or *açorda*, a bread-based soup fragrant with garlic and olive oil and topped by a poached egg.

ON THE ROCKS

A good Madeiran any-time-of-day-snack is *lapas* – grilled limpets served in the shell, each in a puddle of garlic butter which you soak up with plenty of spongy home-made bread: in taste and texture, limpets are very like snails.

WINE, BEER AND SPIRITS

Madeira wine goes very well with desserts, such as *pudim* (cream caramel) or *queijadas da Madeira* (Madeiran cheesecake). You could also try it with *bolo de mel*, the dark molasses-rich cake sold all over Madeira and made from almonds and dried fruits seasoned with cloves, aniseed and fruit peel.

Purists might argue that the best way to sample the four different types of Madeira is to work steadily through the repertoire, starting with dry *sercial* as an aperitif

or accompaniment to fish, then moving on to medium-dry *verdelho* with the main course, and nutty *bual* with dessert, reserving the rich, dark *malvasia* to drink with coffee.

Few Madeirans would drink fortified Madeiran wine with their food, preferring something lighter, such as semi-sparkling *vinho verde* (see below), imported from mainland Portugal, or locally produced red and white wines, which are drunk young, while they are still fresh, fruity and relatively low in alcohol. *Vinho verde* – green wine – is named not for its colour (straw yellow) but for its youthfulness

Also popular as a pick-me-up is *poncha*, a cocktail of sugar-cane spirit, called *aguardente*, mixed with honey and fresh lemon juice.

Coral beer is an excellent light lager-style beer, brewed on the island.

short break

If you have only a short time to visit Madeira and would like to take home some unforgettable memories you can do something local and capture the real flavour of the island. The following suggestions will give you a wide range of sights and experiences that won't take very long, won't cost very much and will make your visit very special.

● **Spend a day in Funchal** (➤ 81–118), with its mosaic-patterned streets, its embroidery shops and its elegant town houses.

● **Step back in time** on a visit to the Adegas de São Francisco wine lodge (➤ 36–37) in Funchal, to learn all about the history of Madeira wine production.

● **Go for dinner in Funchal's Zona Velha** (Old Town, ➤ 54–55) and listen to the plaintive and haunting sound of Portuguese *fado* music.

- **Drive to the top of Pico do Arieiro** (➤ 50–51), Madeira's third highest peak, an hour before dusk to see the scintillating colours of the sunset, or go at night to wonder at the mass of stars in the crystal-clear night sky.

- **Visit the Palheiro Gardens** (➤ 48–49), created by the Blandy family of wine merchants, to see the flowers and shrubs of several continents artfully blended into a fascinating garden.

- **Take a walk** along a *levada* (irrigation canal), penetrating deep into the peaceful heart of the Madeiran countryside.

- **Drive from São Vicente** (➤ 132–133) **to Porto do Moniz** (➤ 125) along the spectacular northern coast, through rock-cut tunnels and beneath waterfalls.

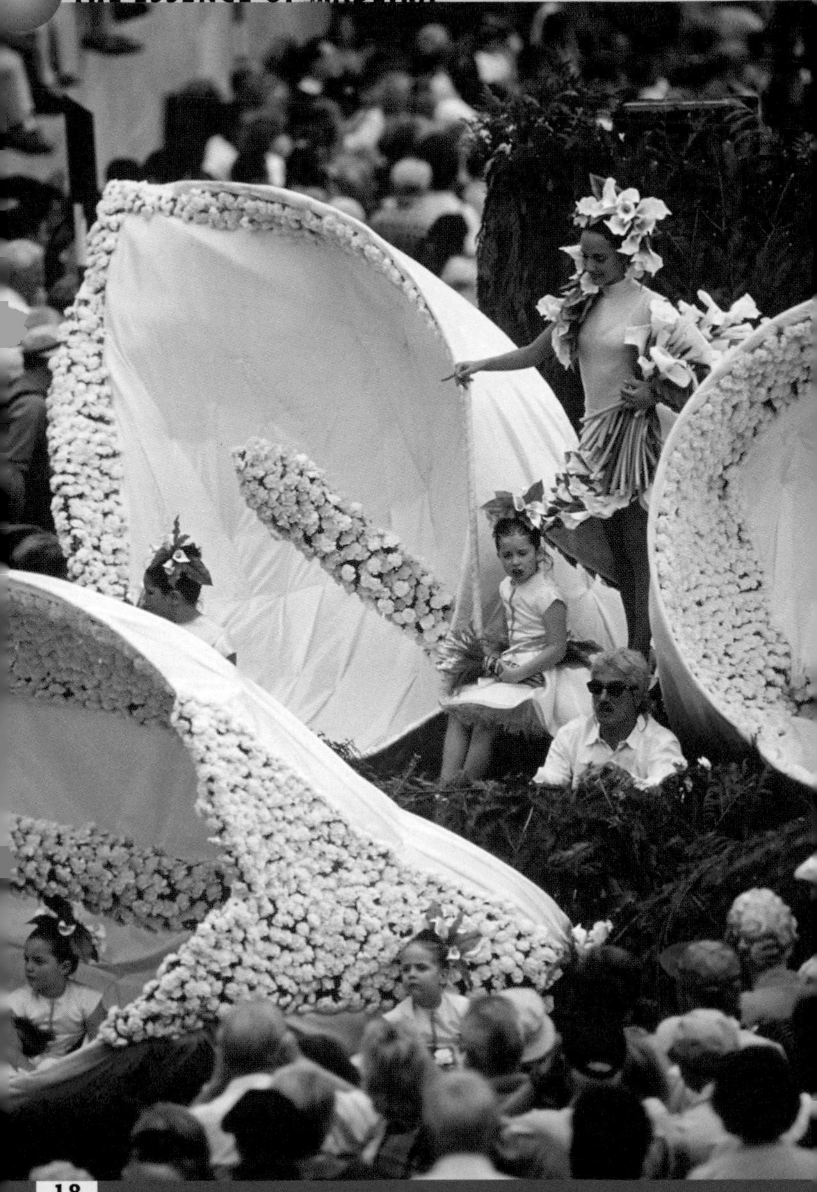

● **Join in a village festivity** for the fun of noisy fireworks and to taste *espetada* (beef kebabs) cooked over an open wood fire.

● **Take a trip to Curral das Freiras** (➤ 40–41) to marvel at the scenic beauty of this hidden valley at the island's heart.

● **Visit the Whaling Museum** (➤ 158) at Caniçal to learn about plans to provide protection for these captivating sea mammals, and loiter on the nearby beach to watch the fishermen land their catch or work on their boats.

Planning

Before you go

WHEN TO GO

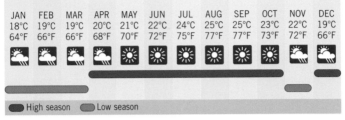

JAN	FEB	MAR	APR	MAY	JUN	JUL	AUG	SEP	OCT	NOV	DEC
18°C	19°C	19°C	20°C	21°C	22°C	24°C	25°C	25°C	23°C	22°C	19°C
64°F	66°F	66°F	68°F	70°F	72°F	75°F	77°F	77°F	73°F	72°F	66°F

● High season ◯ Low season

The temperatures given in the above table are the daily average for each month. Madeira is warm even during the winter, and not too hot in summer. From July to September it can be humid, and it might get too chilly to eat outside at night during November to April, though nights can be just as warm as the days from May to October.

Madeira's weather varies according to the time of day, geography or altitude. For example, it could be very sunny in the morning, raining in the afternoon and then clear in the evening. The southern part of the island tends to have more sun. Between 800 and 1,000m (2,600 and 3,300ft) rain clouds occur, but above these altitudes it is generally clear.

WHAT YOU NEED

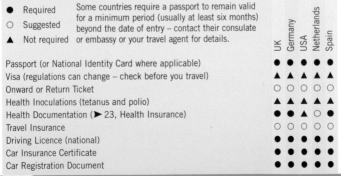

	UK	Germany	USA	Netherlands	Spain
● Required — Some countries require a passport to remain valid for a minimum period (usually at least six months) beyond the date of entry – contact their consulate or embassy or your travel agent for details. ◯ Suggested ▲ Not required					
Passport (or National Identity Card where applicable)	●	●	●	●	●
Visa (regulations can change – check before you travel)	▲	▲	▲	▲	▲
Onward or Return Ticket	◯	◯	◯	◯	◯
Health Inoculations (tetanus and polio)	▲	▲	▲	▲	▲
Health Documentation (▶ 23, Health Insurance)	●	●	▲	◯	●
Travel Insurance	◯	◯	◯	◯	◯
Driving Licence (national)	●	●	●	●	●
Car Insurance Certificate	●	●	●	●	●
Car Registration Document	●	●	●	●	●

WEBSITES

- www.madeiratourism.org
- www.madeiraonline.com
- www.madeira-island.com
- www.madeira-live.com
- www.madeiraguide.com
- www.madeiraislands.travel
- www.madeira-web.com
- www.madeiraarchipelago.com
- www.madeirawineguide.com
- www.themadeiratimes.com

TOURIST OFFICES AT HOME

In the UK

Portuguese National Tourist Office
11 Belgrave Square,
London SW1X 8PP
☎ 020 7201 6666

In the USA

Portuguese National Tourist Office
590 Fifth Avenue, 4th Floor,
New York, NY 10036–4704
☎ 202/354-4403

HEALTH INSURANCE

Insurance Nationals of EU countries can receive free emergency medical treatment on Madeira on production of the relevant documentation (a European Health Insurance Card), although private medical insurance is still advised and is essential for all other visitors. You can apply for an EHIC at the Post Office, online at www.dh.gov.uk/travellers or by calling the EHIC Application Line (tel: 0845 606 2030).

Dental services Dental services on Madeira are generally excellent. Dentists advertise their services in the free English- and German-language magazines available from most hotels and the tourist information centre in Funchal, or just ask at hotel reception.

TIME DIFFERENCES

GMT	Portugal	Germany	USA (NY)	Netherlands	Spain
12 noon	12 noon	1PM	7AM	1PM	1PM

Madeira, like mainland Portugal, observes Greenwich Mean Time (GMT) during the winter months; during the summer, from late March to late September, the time is GMT plus 1 hour.

NATIONAL HOLIDAYS

1 Jan *New Year's Day*
Feb (dates vary)
  Shrove Tuesday and Ash Wednesday
Mar/Apr *Good Friday, Easter Monday*
25 Apr *Day of the Revolution*
1 May *Labour Day*

Jun (date varies) *Corpus Christi*
10 Jun *National Day*
1 Jul *Madeira Day*
15 Aug *Feast of the Assumption*
21 Aug *Funchal Day*
5 Oct *Republic Day*
1 Nov *All Saints' Day*

1 Dec *Restoration of Independence Day*
8 Dec *Immaculate Conception*
25/26 Dec *Christmas*

Most shops, offices and museums close on these days.

WHAT'S ON WHEN

January *Grand New Year Firework Show* (starts midnight 31 Dec): the New Year starts with a bang and noisy blowing of ships' hooters at one of Europe's most spectacular public fireworks festivals.

Dia de Reis (6 Jan): the Day of the Kings, with its religious services and special cakes, marks the end of Christmas and the New Year celebrations.

February *Carnival* (four days before Ash Wednesday): *Carnival* is celebrated all over Madeira, but the costumed parades in Funchal are definitely the best. On the Saturday before Ash Wednesday the highly professional Grand Carnival Parade takes place, when large themed floats,

complete with live bands and up to 150 dancers, form a festive spectacle. On Shrove Tuesday itself, the Public Parade is a chance for local clubs and groups to dress up and compete for prizes.

April *Flower Festival* (second or third weekend): Funchal becomes a blaze of colour for this festival, when shops, houses and churches are all decorated with ribbons and flags, and children make a wall of flowers in Praça do Município. The climax is a parade through Funchal with bands and colourful floats.

June *Fins de Semana Musicais* (all month) Musical Weekends: Madeira's music festival features guest musicians and talented students from the local conservatoire performing in the cathedral and Teatro Baltazar Dias.

August *Feast of the Assumption* (15 Aug): Madeira's biggest religious festival is celebrated with church services by day and dancing, fireworks and feasting by night. Penitents visit the church at Monte to climb the steps on their knees.

September *Madeira Wine Festival* (early Sep): in Funchal and Câmara de Lobos, the completion of the wine harvest is celebrated with public demonstrations of wine-treading, local music and dance and wine tastings.

October *Festa da Macã* (25–26 Oct): the Apple Festival in Camacha offers an opportunity to sample the apples grown around the village, and to enjoy local folk singing and dancing, made more enjoyable by glasses of cider and apple brandy.

November *Festa da Castanha* (1 Nov): the chestnut harvest in Curral das Freiras provides an excuse to consume chestnuts in many forms.

December *Christmas Illuminations* (from 8 Dec): the build-up to Christmas begins when the street illuminations are officially switched on by a local dignitary.

Christmas Cribs (from 16 Dec): the Portuguese tradition of building tableaux representing the crib continues in Funchal, and in many villages.

Village festivals Village festivals celebrate the feast day of the local saint, to whom the parish church is dedicated, or some special event in the history of the village (such as the procession in Machico on 8 October in honour of the crucifix that survived the destruction of the local church).

Getting there

BY AIR
Santa Catarina Airport

22km (13.5 miles) to city centre

🚌 50 minutes

🚗 35 minutes

Most visitors to Madeira arrive by air. Santa Catarina (Funchal) airport is served by scheduled, charter and low-cost flights from most European airports, either direct or via Lisbon. TAP Air Portugal is the national airline (in Funchal tel: 291 213 141).

The airport is 22km (13.5 miles) from the centre of Funchal. Most visitors are met by tour representatives on arrival and their onward transport is generally prearranged. As a result demand for public transport is not great and independent visitors may have to take a taxi to the centre of Funchal (around 35 minutes). The alternative is the airport bus, which departs at roughly 90-minute intervals and takes around 50 minutes.

Getting around

PUBLIC TRANSPORT

Internal flights There are several flights a day from Funchal to Porto Santo. The 37km (23-mile) journey takes 15 minutes, and flights are heavily booked in high season, so be sure to reserve well in advance. Flights can be reserved through any travel agent or through branches of TAP Air Portugal. On Madeira TAP's office is at Avenida das Comunidades Madeirenses 10 (tel: 291 213 141).

Buses A highly efficient bus system connects all towns with Funchal. Buses are modern and comfortable (though they do not have safety belts) and most drivers take care to drive safely on Madeira's tortuous roads.

Buses within Funchal and its suburbs are painted orange; those serving the rural areas are operated by five different companies, each with its own livery. Nearly all buses depart from the bus stops along Avenida do Mar, where you can also buy tickets from the bus company kiosks (7-day go-as-you-please passes are available to visitors only, so bring your passport if you want to buy one). Up-to-date timetables can be bought from the tourist office on Avenida Arriaga.

Boat trips to Porto Santo A sleek cruise ship promises smooth sailings and many onboard facilities; the journey time is 2 hours 40 minutes. Tickets can be bought in advance from travel agents, or from the office of the Porto Santo Line, Rua da Praia 6, Funchal (tel: 291 210 300).

Several cruise companies operate out of Funchal's yachting marina, all offering half- or full-day excursions around Madeira's coastline. Turipesca (tel: 291 231 063) operates charter cruises, game-fishing trips and regular cruises (including evening cruises with dinner).

TAXIS

There are taxi ranks in towns and taxis may also stop if flagged down, especially in the countryside. Rates for out-of-town journeys (eg from Funchal to the airport) are fixed. Short journeys are metered. For longer journeys, you can negotiate an hourly or half-day rate.

DRIVING

- Drive on the right.
- Speed limit on motorways: 110kph (68mph)
  Speed limit on main roads: 80kph (50mph)
  Speed limit on urban roads: 60 or 40kph (37 or 25mph)
- It is mandatory for drivers and passengers to wear seat belts if fitted.
- Random breath-testing takes place. Never drive under the influence of alcohol.
- Petrol *(gasolina)* comes in two grades: lead-free *(sem chumbo)* and lead-substitute *(super)*. Diesel *(gasóleo)* is also available. Most villages and towns have a petrol station, and they are generally open from 8 to 8. The GALP petrol station on Avenida do Infante, in Funchal, is open 24 hours. Most take credit cards.
- Because all visitors to Madeira drive rental cars, there is no central breakdown and rescue service. Instead, the car rental companies operate their own breakdown services, with repairs usually being carried out promptly. The documents you are given on renting the car will explain what to do in the event of a breakdown.
- It is obligatory to have your headlights on while you are driving on motorways.

CAR RENTAL

The major car rental firms are represented on Madeira, as well as several local companies, which offer competitive rates. You can reserve a car in advance through travel agents, at the airport on arrival or through your hotel. All rental firms will deliver your car to you.

FARES AND CONCESSIONS

In Funchal, the main bus stops and ticket kiosks are on Avenida do Mar (the saefront). You must cancel your ticket as you board the bus. Seven-day passes, available on all routes , are available to visitors, but there are no concessions. It must be remembered that Madeiran public transport is timetables to the needs of the local people, not visitors.

Students and children pay lower rates for admission to museums and atrtractions – bring a passport or student card as proof of age.

Being there

TOURIST OFFICES
Funchal Avenida Arriaga 16
☎ 291 211 900
Machico Forte de Nossa Senhora
do Amparo ☎ 291 962 289
Porto Santo Avenida Dr Manuel

Grégorio Pestana Júnior
☎ 291 985 189
Ribeira Brava Forte de Sâo Bento
☎ 291 951 675
Santana Sítio do Serrado
☎ 291 572 992

Some travel agencies in Funchal advertise themselves as if they were tourist information centres, though their primary aim is to sell you one of their organized tours. In general these tours (by mini bus or coach) are good value and the standards of safety are high. You must expect, however, that the tour will include time spent in shops and restaurants rather than sightseeing – you may prefer the flexibility of your own taxi with driver, which can work out as cheap as an organized tour if several people share a car.

MONEY
Portugal's currency is the euro (€), divided into 100 cents. Coins come in denominations of 1, 2, 5, 10, 20 and 50 cents and 1 and 2 euros. Notes come in denominations of 5, 10, 20, 50, 100 and 500 euros (the last two are rarely seen). MasterCard, Visa, American Express and Diners cards

TIPS/GRATUITIES

Yes ✓ No ✗		
Restaurants (service and tax included)	✓	10%
Bar service	✓	change
Taxis	✓	10%
Porters	✓	€1.50
Chambermaids	✗	
Tour guides	✓	€5
Toilets	✗	

are widely accepted, as are travellers' cheques. Banks with exchange bureaux are found in Funchal and the larger towns. Commission on changing euro travellers' cheques can be high; it pays to look around.

POSTAL AND INTERNET SERVICES

Post offices *(Correios)* are found in the main towns (open Mon–Fri 8:30–8, Sat 9–12:30). In Funchal, the most central one is on Avenida do Zarco. Poste restante services are available at the main post office on Rua Dr Joao Brito Camara. Stamps can also be bought from many newsagents.

Most hotels offer some form of internet connection, usually a 'client' machine in a corner of a public room. This is often free, so in demand. WiFi connection is also offered, using preprinted cards purchased at reception. Use of telephone internet connection from your room is very costly.

TELEPHONES

Telephones are found in cafés and on streets in larger towns. Some only take phonecards, available from newsagents and cafés. To call Madeira or Porto Santo from abroad dial 00 351 (the international code for Portugal) then 291 (the area code for both islands).

Emergency telephone numbers
Police 112   **Ambulance** 112
Fire 112

International dialling codes
From Madeira (Portugal) to: **USA and Canada** 00 1
UK 00 44   **Netherlands** 00 31
Germany 00 49   **Spain** 00 34

CONSULATES
UK ☎ 291 212 860   **USA** ☎ 291 235 636
Germany ☎ 291 220 338   **Netherlands** ☎ 291 703 803

ELECTRICITY

The power supply on Madeira is: 220 volts AC. Sockets accept continental two-pronged plugs, so an adaptor is needed for non-continental appliances, and a transformer for devices operating on 100–120 volts.

HEALTH AND SAFETY

Sun advice The sun can be intense on Madeira at any time of the year, and it is possible to burn with less than an hour's exposure. If you are out walking on bare mountains, it is best to cover vulnerable parts of your body, including your neck, legs and arms.

Drugs Chemists *(farmâcia)* are open Mon–Fri 9–1, 3–7, Sat 9–12:30. Some open through the lunch break, and there is a late-night duty rota, posted in pharmacy windows. Take supplies of any drugs that you take regularly, since there is no guarantee that they will be available locally.

Safe water Tap water is safe to drink everywhere. Mineral water is readily available; fizzy water *(água com gás)*, rather than still *(água sem gás)*, is likely to be naturally sparkling, rather than carbonated.

Crime Incidents are extremely rare, but in the unlikely event that you are the victim of theft, report your loss to the main police station at the Rua Dr João de Deus 7 (tel: 291 222 022) and get a copy of the written statement in order to support your insurance claim.

- Leave your valuables in the hotel.
- Do not leave valuables in cars.
- Do not leave unattended valuables on the beach or poolside.
- Beware of pickpockets in markets and on crowded streets.

OPENING HOURS

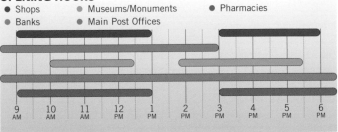

- Shops
- Banks
- Museums/Monuments
- Main Post Offices
- Pharmacies

9 AM 10 AM 11 AM 12 PM 1 PM 2 PM 3 PM 4 PM 5 PM 6 PM

Small shops are open Mon–Sat 9 or 10–7 or 8. Some close early on Saturday and only those aimed at tourists open on Sunday. Larger stores and supermarkets are open daily 10–10. Pharmacies open late on a duty rota (posted on pharmacy doors). Village post offices have shorter opening hours; main post offices also open Saturday morning.

LANGUAGE

Portuguese is the language of Madeira, but most hoteliers, shopkeepers and restaurateurs speak English and German as well. Portuguese is easy to understand in its written form if you already know a Romance language – such as Latin, French, Italian or Spanish.

yes/no	*sim/não*	good evening/night	*boa noite*
please	*faz favor*	excuse me	*desculpe*
thank you (m/f)	*obrigado/a*	you're welcome	*está bem*
hello/goodbye	*olá/adeus*	do you speak	*fala inglês?*
good morning	*bom dia*	English?	
good afternoon	*boa tarde*	I don't understand	*não compreendo*
bank	*um banco*	pounds/dollars	*ulibras/dólares*
exchange office	*câmbios*	credit card	*cartão de crédito*
post office	*correio*	traveller's cheque	*cheque de viagem*
coins/banknotes	*moedas/notas*	cheque	*cheque*
receipt	*recibo*	how much?	*quanta custa?*
breakfast	*pequeno almoço*	bill	*conta*
lunch/dinner	*almoço/jontar*	beer	*cerveja*
table	*mesa*	menu	*lista*
starter	*entrada*	red wine	*vinho tinto*
main course	*prato principal*	white wine	*vinho branco*
dessert	*sobremesa*	water	*água*
hotel	*hotel/estalagem*	twin room	*quarto com*
do you have a room?	*tem um quarto livre?*		*duascamas*
I have a reservation	*tenho um quarto reservado*	with bathroom	*com banho*
		one night	*um noite*
a single room	*um quarto simples*	key	*chave*
double room	*quarto de casal*	sea view	*vista a mar*
aeroplane/airport	*avião/aeroporto*	single/return	*ida/ide e volta*
bus/bus station	*autocarro/estação de autocarros*	how far?	*a que distância?*
		where is?	*onde está?*
a ticket to	*um bilhete para*	petrol	*gasolina*

Best places to see

1 Adegas de São Francisco

Visit a wine lodge set in a medieval monastery to sample Madeira and learn how it is produced.

To step from the bustle of Funchal's main street into the calm courtyards of the Adegas de São Francisco is to enter a world where time has a different meaning. Here, on payment of a fairly substantial sum, you can buy wines that were bottled in the 1860s, while upstairs, slowly maturing in huge barrels of Brazilian satinwood and American oak, are wines that nobody living today is likely to taste. As Churchill said, 'to drink Madeira is to sip history with every glass'.

The lodge, with its romantic timber buildings and wisteria-hung balconies, started life as the monastery of St Francis and was converted to its present use in 1834. At that time, Madeira wines were still being sent on board ship to the equator and back in the belief that the rocking motion

improved the wine. The production process was revolutionised by the accidental discovery that Madeira's unique quality comes not from motion but from gentle heating. Now the wine is 'cooked' in vast vats using the warmth of the sun, boosted when necessary by the heat from hot water pipes. All this becomes clear as you tour the cobbled yard to see ancient wooden presses and leather-bound wine ledgers, learn the subtle arts of the wine blender and visit the warming rooms, with their deliciously heady smell of old wood and wine. Scents such as these are a prelude to the pleasures to come as you head for the sampling that concludes this popular tour, which takes place in a room with delightful murals painted in 1922 by Max Römer.

✚ *Funchal 2c* ✉ Avenida Arriaga 28, Funchal ☎ 291 740 110 🕐 Mon–Fri 9:30–6:30, Sat 10–1. Guided tours: Mon–Fri 10:30, 2:30, 3:30, 4:30, Sat 11. 'Vintage Experience' tours Wed, Fri 4:30. Closed Sun, public hols ✋ Moderate 🍴 Theatre café (€) opposite
ℹ Avenida Arriaga 16 ☎ 291 211 900

2 Cabo Girão

The towering cliff face of Cabo Girão can be viewed from a boat or from the dizzy heights of its clifftop balcony.

Cabo Girão is not quite Europe's highest sea cliff, but at 580m (1,902ft) it is impressive enough. Girão means 'turning', an apt description of the vertiginous effect of looking down to the sea from the clifftop. In fact, it is said that the name dates from Zarco's first voyage of discovery when he set out to explore the Madeiran coast in 1420. His diary vividly describes sailing 'towards a dark, stupendous object … abode of demons and evil spirits'. Deciding to venture no further, Zarco turned back at this point to seek a safe anchorage at what is now the fishing port of Câmara de Lobos (► 138–139).

For a different view of Cabo Girão you can retrace Zarco's voyage by taking a boat excursion along Madeira's southern coast. Numerous companies offer tours from Funchal, and you can either book direct by visiting the marina, or through hotels and travel agents. Half-day tours go as far west as Ponta do Sol (► 124), and most operators anchor off Cabo Girão so that you can dive off the boat and swim in the clean, warm waters. One company, Turipesca, also offers fishing trips.

Alternatively, if you have a good head for heights, you can take a cable car down the face of the cliff to the beach at its base, where brave and hardy farmers cultivate vines on handkerchief-sized plots, taking advantage of the warmth stored in these south-facing rocks.

✚ 16M ✉ 22km (13.5 miles) west of Funchal, and 10km (6 miles) west of Câmara de Lobos 🍴 Snack bar (€) alongside the viewing platform 🚍 Bus 154 from Funchal 🚢 Details of boat excursions from companies based in the yacht marina, such as Turipesca (☎ 291 231 063) and Costa do Sol (☎ 291 238 538) ❓ For the cable car take the Fajãs turning off Via Rápida after Câmara de Lobos and follow signs for 'Teleférico' ☎ 291 944 248

3 Curral das Freiras

This secret valley, known as the Nuns' Corral (or Refuge), is hidden among the peaks of Madeira's central mountain range.

Only with mild exaggeration did H N Coleridge, nephew of the poet, describe Curral das Freiras (the name literally means Nuns' Refuge) as 'one of the great sights of the world'. The majestic peaks that encircle the village certainly invite such claims, though quiet contemplation of the views can sometimes be difficult because of the sheer number of visitors in high season. If you prefer relative solitude, the best way to find it is to walk into the village along the old zig-zag path that starts at Eira do Serrado (Eagle's Nest), high above the village, parking alongside the café, shop and hotel.

Until 1959, this cobbled path was the only way in and out of the village. Its impregnability was the reason why the nuns of Santa Clara Convent (➤ 82) fled here in 1566 to escape from piratical raids on Funchal. Even if you don't want to walk all the way down, it is still

worth stopping at Eira do Serrado in order to enjoy the plummeting views from the lookout point (Miradouro) located just a short walk from the hotel. From here, the village far below seems to sit in the bowl of a vast crater, surrounded by sheer cliffs rising to jagged peaks. The view is not quite so enthralling from the bottom looking up, but there are other compensations: bars in Curral das Freiras sell the local speciality, a delicious chestnut-flavoured liqueur called *licor de castanha*, as well as bread, soup and cakes made from chestnuts, all of which are harvested in autumn from trees growing in woods all around the village.

🕂 17J ✉ 20km (12.5 miles) northwest of Funchal 🖐 Free 🍴 Nuns' Valley Restaurant (€) in the centre of the village 🚌 Bus 81 from Funchal

4 Mercado dos Lavradores, Funchal

The covered market in Funchal is a full of colourful island produce, a great place to shop for fruit, flowers and souvenirs.

The Workers' Market was built in 1937 as a producers' market, where island farmers and fishermen could bring their produce for sale direct to the public. Now professional retailers predominate, but the original spirit prevails on Friday, as farmers from the remotest corners of Madeira descend on Funchal in loaded-down pick-up trucks to sell their home-grown produce.

Flower-sellers in traditional island costume have colonised the entrance to the market. Their stalls sell keenly priced cut flowers and bulbs – tubs full of amaryllis bulbs, freshly dug and smelling of earth, or delicate orchid blooms might tempt you to buy a souvenir of the island's horticultural richness.

In the fish hall, there are scenes to turn the stomach. If the razor-sharp teeth and large staring eyes of the scabbard fish do not give you nightmares, the sight of huge tuna fish being gutted and filleted may well.

For pleasanter sights and fragrances, head for the upper floor, with its lavish displays of seasonal fruit and vegetables. If you are self-catering on Madeira, you could do worse than come here to buy good fresh food.

🔡 *Funchal 4b* ✉ Rua Dr Fernão Ornelas 🕐 Mon–Thu 7–4, Fri 7–8, Sat 7–5. Closed Sun 🍴 Many stalls selling snacks, plus bars and pavement cafés in the nearby Zona Velha

5 The Monte Toboggan Ride

The quintessential Madeira experience is to slide in a metal-shod toboggan down the steep cobbled streets linking Monte to Funchal.

Was Ernest Hemingway being ironic when he described the Monte toboggan ride as one of the most exhilarating experiences of his life? The only way to find out is to try it for yourself by heading up to the hill town of Monte, high above Funchal. Here you can join the line of apprehensive travellers queuing to slide back down to the capital in a wicker basket mounted on polished metal runners. Two toboggan drivers, wearing rubber-soled boots for grip, will push and steer you over the polished streets and ensure that you do not come to grief as you negotiate sharp bends.

The ride ends in the suburb of Livramento, some 2km (1.2 miles) downhill, where taxis await. Some visitors consider this brief but unique journey to be the highlight of their visit to Madeira – others consider it overpriced hype (as well as the price of the ride, you will be expected to tip the toboggan drivers, and pay for the souvenir photographs that are taken as you descend and presented to you at the journey's end).

🚏 19L ✉ Toboggan rides start from the foot of the steps of Nossa Senhora do Monte church 🕐 Toboggan rides are available Mon–Sat 9–6, Sun 9–1 ✋ Expensive 🍴 Café (€) frequented by toboggan drivers alongside church steps 🚌 Town bus 20, 21, 22 or Teleféricos da Madeiras (➤ 54)

6 Museu de Arte Sacra, Funchal

Enjoy masterpieces of Flemish art, paid for by Madeira's highly profitable sugar trade with northern Europe.

Funchal's Sacred Art Museum is housed in the former bishop's palace, built in 1600 and given its gracious cobbled courtyard and entrance staircase when the building was remodelled between 1748 and 1757. Displayed on the first floor is a collection of ancient religious vestments, silverware and statuary collected from remote churches all over Madeira. Some of these objects date to the earliest years of the island's colonization, including the intricately decorated processional cross donated to Funchal Cathedral by the Portuguese King Manuel I, who reigned from 1490 to 1520.

The best of the museum's treasures are displayed on the upper floor. Here you can enjoy the naturalism and human pathos of several beautiful painted wooden statues of the Virgin and Child, as well as the warm colours of several fine Flemish masterpieces. For many years it was not known who painted these remarkable pictures of the Nativity, the Crucifixion and of various saints. By comparison with works by known artists, scholars have now deduced that they are principally the work of leading painters based in Bruges and Antwerp in the late 15th and early 16th centuries, including Gerard David (1468–1523), Dieric Bouts (died 1475) and Jan Provost (1465–1529). Several paintings include portraits of the donors, wealthy merchants who made a fortune from the Madeiran sugar trade. One fine example shows an Italian merchant, Simon Acciaiuoli, kneeling at prayer with his Scottish wife, Mary Drummond, in a painting of the *Descent from the Cross*, while another shows Simon Gonçalves da Câmara, the grandson of Zarco, Madeira's discoverer, and his family.

✚ *Funchal 3b* ✉ Rua do Bispo 21 ☎ 291 228 900 🕐 Tue–Sat 10–12:30, 2:20–6, Sun 10–1. Closed Mon, public hols 🍴 Café do Museu (€) at rear of museum

7 Palheiro, Jardims do

The botanical riches of Africa, Asia and the Americas are combined in the beautifully landscaped gardens of this aristocratic estate.

Of all the gardens on Madeira, those surrounding the Quinta do Palheiro Ferreiro (originally known as Blandy's Gardens) are the most rewarding. Here the spirit of the English garden has been transposed to Madeira, where full advantage has been taken of the frost-free environment. Plants that would curl up and die further north, or which have to be cosseted in the hothouse, thrive here out of doors. To create this lovely garden, successive generations of the Blandy family have been able to draw on the limitless treasures of the botanical world, planting gorgeous proteas from southern Africa, flame-flowered climbers from southern America,

sweetly scented Japanese flowering shrubs, and Chinese trees with exotically patterned bark. The result is a garden full of surprises and unexpected plant combinations.

The English influence is evident in the division of the garden into a series of 'rooms' divided by hedges and linked by mixed borders. Smaller intimate areas, such as the peaceful and shaady Ladies' Garden, with its topiary peacocks, give way to more open areas, such as the sweeping lawns surrounding the baroque chapel built by the Count of Carvalhal.

The wealthy count was the original owner of this estate, which the Blandy family acquired in 1885. Part of the estate remains exactly as the count laid it out in the late 18th century, including the stately avenue of gnarled old plane trees that leads up to his original mansion. Beyond the mansion is an extensive area of informal woodland, signposted 'Inferno' (Hell), where blue morning glory vines trail among primeval tree ferns from New Zealand.

✚ 20L ✉ São Gonçalo, 8km (5 miles) east of Funchal ☎ 291 793 044 🕑 Mon–Fri 9–4:30. Closed Sat, Sun 💰 Moderate 🍴 Tea House (€) 🚌 Town bus 36, 37

8 Pico do Arieiro

**Drive to the top of
Madeira's third highest
peak for raw volcanic
landscapes and
spectacular views, best
enjoyed at sunset or
sunrise.**

Pico do Arieiro (1,818m/
5,965ft) is the third highest peak
on Madeira. It is easily reached
from central Funchal by driving
north on the winding EN 103
road to Poiso, and then taking
the EN 202 west.

As you climb above Poiso, the
green woodland that cloaks
much of central Madeira gives
way to a wilder upland
landscape of sheep-grazed turf.
The sense of travelling to a
different world is reinforced by
the cloud belt, which often
hangs at around 1,200m
(3,900ft). Passing through this,
you emerge in brilliant sunshine.
Bare rock soon becomes the
predominant feature in the
landscape, and only the hardiest
of plants can find any toehold
among the clinker-like tufa that
makes up the summit of Pico
do Arieiro.

To compensate for the lack of vegetation, there are tremendous views over an endless succession of knife-edge ridges and sheer cliffs. Cotton-wool clouds hang in the valleys far below and the only sound comes from the wind. The predominant colours are purple, burnt orange and chocolate brown, a reminder of Madeira's volcanic origins. The rocks are even more vividly colourful when lit by the red and orange rays of the setting sun, or the pink light of dawn.

✠ 18J 🍴 Snack bar (€)

9 Sé (Funchal Cathedral)

Founded in 1485, Funchal's cathedral is one of Madeira's oldest buildings and a link with the island's original settlers.

Portugal's King Manuel I was so proud of his newly acquired island province that, in 1485, he decided to send one of Lisbon's top architects, Pedro Enes, to build a new cathedral for Funchal. The result, completed in 1514, is essentially a sombre building, although it is enlivened with Arabic-style architectural details. The most lavish exterior decoration is found not around the entrance portal, as is customary, but at the east end of the church, where the roofline is decorated with pinnacles shaped like miniature minarets. These echo the

shape of the spire, which is covered in glazed *azulejos* (tiles) that were originally intended to protect the structure from wind and rain, rather than act as decoration. The comparatively plain portal bears King Manuel I's coat of arms at the top, incorporating the red cross of the Knights Templar, of which Manuel was the Grand Master.

The cool interior of the cathedral reveals its secrets only slowly as your eyes adapt to the darkness. High above the nave is a carved wooden ceiling inlaid with geometric designs in ivory. If you look long enough, or use binoculars, you will begin

to make out strange animals and exotic flowers among the designs. Easier to appreciate are the choir stalls, boldly carved with near-lifesize figures of the Apostles, painted in gold against a background of powder blue. The Apostles are dressed in stylish hats, cloaks, tunics, boots and belts, giving us a good idea of the kind of clothes worn by prosperous Madeiran sugar merchants when the stalls were carved in the early 16th century. More entertaining scenes from contemporary life are to be found carved on the undersides of the choir seats. As well as cherubs, you will find monkeys and pigs and a porter carrying a pigskin full of wine.

✚ *Funchal 3c* ✉ Largo da Sé ☎ 291 228 155 🕐 Mon–Sat 9–12:30, 4–5:30 (services early morning and early evening) ✋ Free 🍴 Many pavement cafés (€) on cathedral square

10 Zona Velha (Old Town), Funchal

For atmosphere, inexpensive food and authentic Portuguese *fado* music, Funchal's Zona Velha is the best place to head.

Funchal's Zona Velha (Old Town), formerly the city's slum, is now an area of cobbled streets with craft shops occupying the low, one-roomed houses where at one time whole families slept, ate and played. The former boatyard has been filled in to create the base station for the Teleféricos da Madeiras (Madeira Cable Car), while opposite the station is the Madeira Story Centre (➤ 89–91), a great place to go at the beginning of your visit to Madeira to gain a sense of the island's history. At the eastern end, under the walls of the Fortaleza de São Tiago (➤ 84), there is a tiny black-pebble beach (the Praia da Barreirinha) where

local people still come to bathe and eat grilled sardines sold by street vendors. The Old Town's last remaining fishermen also repair their boats here.

The beach remains popular despite the new lido, complete with swimming pools and sea-bathing facilities, just beyond the fortress. Opposite the lido stands the Igreja do Socorro (also called Santa Maria Maior), rebuilt several times since it was founded in the 16th century in thanksgiving for the ending of an epidemic. By contrast, the tiny Capela do Corpo Santo, in the heart of the old town, remains a simple 16th-century fishermen's chapel.

Surrounding the chapel are pavement cafés and restaurants that make the Zona Velha the bustling heart of Funchal's nightlife. Many restaurants specialize in fresh fish, and it is to here that Portuguese holiday-makers come for *bacalhau* (salt cod) or *arroz de mariscos* (seafood risotto). Arsénio's restaurant (➤ 58, 118) offers nightly performances of *fado* music, that strangely plaintive and addictive import from Lisbon in which the singer bemoans their star-crossed fate. When Arsénio's closes, the *fado* entourage moves to the bar round the corner.

✚ *Funchal 5c* ✉ Located in the eastern part of the city 🍴 Some of the city's best restaurants are here (€–€€)

Best things to do

Good places to have lunch

Arsénio's (€€)
Good local food. Come for dinner and there's *fado* music as well.
✉ Rua de Santa Maria 169, Funchal ☎ 291 224 007

Café Arco-Velha (€)
Enjoy a simple but satisfying lunch of limpets and grilled sardines at this Old Town restaurant and watch the world go by from its pavement tables.
✉ Rua de Carlos I 42, Funchal ☎ 291 225 683

Café do Museum (€)
The glassed-in Renaissance arcade at the rear of the Museu de Arte Sacra (Sacred Art Museum) offers grandstand views of Funchal's main square.
✉ Praça do Município, Funchal ☎ 291 228 900

Café do Teatro (€)
Chic young Funchalese poseurs and artistic types come here, with the aim of being seen by their friends. Cool black and white décor and a cobbled patio garden.
✉ Teatro Baltazar Dias, Avenida Arriaga, Funchal ☎ 291 249 959

Golden Gate (€)
A great café for people-watching, with outside tables under the jacaranda trees of the city's main drag.
✉ Avenida Arriaga 24–29, Funchal ☎ 291 234 383

Hortensia Gardens Tea House (€)
Although it's served by town bus 47, most visitors stumble across this tea house as they walk the Levada dos Tornos and are grateful for its warm welcome, home cooked soups, salads, scones and waffles, and beautiful garden.
✉ Caminho dos Pretos 89, São Gonçalo, Funchal ☎ 291 792 179

Jasmin Tea House (€)

The lazy way to get to this house in the woods is to take a taxi or bus 47. Most visitors come here by walking from the Palheiro Gardens (at the garden exit turn right, follow the estate wall uphill, turn left in the village and walk up about 100m/110yds to a white garage, then turn left up a track to the *levada* path). Follow the *levada* path for 25 minutes through eucalyptus woods and you will work up an appetite to enjoy the homemade salads, soups and sandwiches served here at lunchtime – or the cream teas.

✉ Quinta da Ribeira, Caminho dos Pretos 40, São Gonçalo, Funchal
☎ 291 792 796

Nuns' Valley Café (€)

Lunch with one of Madeira's finest views: chestnuts are the local speciality so try chestnut bread or soup (and chestnut liqueur for those who are not driving).

✉ Curral das Freiras (opposite the church) ☎ 291 712 177

Vagrant (Beatles' Boat) (€€)

Spoil your children with lunch on this novelty boat and try explaining to them who the Beatles were, and why they were important.

✉ Avenida das Comunidades Madeirenses, Funchal ☎ 291 223 572

Stunning views

The Eira do Serrado above Curral das Freiras (➤ 40, 41)

The clifftops at Ponta de São Lourenço (➤ 162–163)

Places to take the children

Aquaparque
Tubes, slides and a choice of paddling and bathing pools make this the best water park on the island.

✉ Ribeira do Boaventura (just west of Santa Cruz) ☎ 291 324 412 🕓 Daily 10–7 (to 7:30 in summer)

Dolphin-watching
The boat operators who lead these trips usually know where to look. Trips take place most days (weather permitting), leaving from Funchal's Marina at 10.30, 3 and 6.15. Further details from Gavião Madeira (☎ 291 241 124) or Venturado Mar (☎ 291 280 033).

Football
Madeira has two first-division football teams: C S Marítimo (Estádio dos Barreiros, north of the Hotel Zone) and Nacional (Estádio de Choupana, in the hills above Funchal). Home matches are played on alternate Sundays in the season.

☎ Tourist office 291 211 902

Grutas e Centro do Volcanismo de São Vicente
The top attraction for children on Madeira is this cave system just north of São Vicentes. However, the guided tour is so short you spend only 15–20 minutes inside the caves. The audiovisuals and exhibitions extend the total time to one hour.

✉ Sítio do Pé do Passo, São Vicente ☎ 291 842 404 🕓 Apr–Sep daily 9–9; Oct–Mar daily 9–7 💰 Expensive

Parque Temático da Madeira
A ride through stormy seas on board Zarco's ship, simulations of paragliding over Madeira's cliffs and peaks and fascinating displays on the island's history and culture, as well as a boating lake and adventure playgrounds (► 149).

✉ Fonte da Pedra, just off main Santana to São Jorge road ☎ 291 570 410
🕓 Daily 10–7. Closed Mon mid-Sep to early Dec, mid-Jan to end 1 Jun

Good places to swim

Aquaparque (➤ 62, 169)

The Lido (➤ 73)

Porto Santo – one huge stretch of golden sand (➤ 175–186)

Prainha, Madeira's sandiest beach (➤ 165)

The rock pools at Porto do Moniz (➤ 125)

The Quinta do Magnólia gardens (➤ 73)

The Savoy Resort (➤ 105)

Peace and quiet

Downtown Funchal can be as frenetic and bustling as any major holiday destination, but on Madeira it is easy to find a little peace and quiet to enjoy a few magic moments that will hallmark you Madeiran experience for years to come.

Stroll beside a *levada*

Ribeiro Frio (► 144–145) is a delightful mountain village, and from it an entirely level path runs alongside a *levada* (irrigation canal) to Balcões; there's no need to hurry, just amble along, you can't go wrong – and there's a café along the way. The path leads through rock cuttings to a spectacular viewpoint over mountain peaks and pinnacles that could so easily be Patagonia or the Andes. Come back the same way; it's only 3km (2 miles) in total.

Visit Poiso

This crossing point between north and south Madeira boasts a bar-hotel-restaurant, but the way to Poiso (➤ 50) from Funchal climbs through shady eucalyptus forest, fragrant with menthol, sun-dappled clearings where butterflies feed, banks of wild hydrangeas and agapanthus, rural farms, orchards and waterfalls. There is a large picnic area en route where you can get off the road and enjoy an alfresco lunch.

Lizard lore

As you walk around the Madeiran countryside, rustlings in the undergrowth may take you by surprise. The chances are that if the noise is not from a grazing goat, it is caused by one of the island's ubiquitous lizards. Varying in colour from basalt black to bright green, they can grow up to 17cm (6.5 inches) in length. Farmers regard them as a mixed blessing: although they help to keep down pests, they also like to feed on the grapes and soft fruit growing in the island's vineyards and orchards.

Top activities

***Levada* walking:** it is what makes Madeira different and special (► 64); buy the Sunflower or Cicerone walking guides for lots of ideas.

Being botanical: you cannot visit Madeira without being bowled over by nature's profusion; buy a guide to the flora of the island and discover the names of all those beautiful flowering trees.

Wine tasting: take advantage of the free tastings offered by many wine shops and cellars.

Keeping fit: many people come to Madeira just to keep fit by swimming and playing tennis, making the most of the hotel sports facilities.

Shopping for embroidery: even if you decide you cannot afford that gorgeous embroidered blouse, or that lovely nightdress, you can at least dream. Be sure that what you buy is authentic.

Sailing: surrounded by water, Madeira is the ideal place to enjoy a short coastal voyage.

Diving: learn to dive with Madeira Divepoint, based in the Pestana Carlton hotel (☎ 291 239 579; www.madeiradivepoint.com) or the Diving Centre Cachalote, based in the Crowne Plaza hotel in Funchal (☎ 291 717 642; ► 102).

Golf: Madeira has two of Europe's most scenic links: the Madeira Golf Club at Santo da Serra (☎ 291 550 100; www.santodaserragolf.com) and the Quinta do Palheiro Golf Club (☎ 291 790 126; www.palheirogolf.com).

Tobogganing: sail across the rooftops of Funchal on the Monte cable car, then descend on the traditional toboggan (► 44–45).

a walk

around the harbour

Early evening is a good time to do this walk, ending up with a view from a pavement café of Madeira's brief sunset.

Start at the tourist office in Avenida Arriaga and turn right.

Funchal's residents gather to chat in the tree-shaded Jardim de São Francisco, near the Adegas de São Francisco wine lodge (► 36–37). Opposite is the remarkable 1920s Toyota showroom, decorated with tile pictures of the Monte toboggan (► 44–45). Close by is the Municipal Theatre of 1888 (you can go and look inside if there is no performance) and the trendy theatre bar, with its own tree-shaded patio, alongside.

Turn left beside the theatre, down Rua do Conselheiro José Silvestre Ribeiro.

At the bottom, on the left, is the Casa do Turista, an elegantly furnished town house packed with quality products from Madeira and mainland Portugal.

Turn right, if you wish, to walk through the busy port and out along the Molhe da Pontinha, the great sea wall that encloses the harbour where cruise liners dock. Alternatively, cross to the sea wall side of Avenida do Mar and turn left.

The 16th-century Palaçio de São Lourenço, on your left, bristles with ancient cannon. To your right is the yacht marina, enclosed by a high sea wall painted by visiting sailors with pictures recording their visit. Seafood restaurants line the landward side, and ice-cream booths and floating restaurants lie further up along Avenida do

Mar. Beyond, on the left, is the Madeiran Regional Parliament, with its circular modern debating chamber.

Turn left up the street just before this building to reach the cathedral square (➤ 52–53), with its many pavement cafés.

Distance 1.5km (1 mile)
Time 1 hour
Start point Tourist Information Centre, Avenida Arriaga 18
✚ *Funchal 2c*
End point Largo da Sé ✚ *Funchal 3c*
Lunch Marina Terrace (€€) ✉ Marina do Funchal ☎ 291 230 547

Best souvenirs and shopping

SOUVENIRS

Antiques
The streets leading up to São Pedro church have several shops selling old maps and engravings, wooden chests, gilded chandeliers, mirrors with fine old frames, oriental spice jars, furniture and clocks.

Embroidery
Madeiran embroidery is made by hand and it takes many hours to produce even a simple napkin – hence the high prices. It is distinguished from machine-made products (mostly from the Far East) by the special lead seal (or hologram) attached to each piece after it has been inspected for quality and finish, a guarantee of authenticity. It is worth visiting a factory before you make your final purchase.

Leatherwork
Portuguese leatherwork is renowned throughout Europe. Madeira has a number of shops selling beautifully made goods at half the price they would fetch in Paris, London or Rome.

Tapestry
Herbert Kiekeben, a German artist, introduced the craft of sewing pictures on canvas to Madeira in 1938. Though it has not outgrown embroidery in the Madeiran craft league, locally made products now sell worldwide.

Wine and liqueurs

The most enjoyable way to buy wine is to visit a wine lodge, where you can sample the products. Take a tour of the Adegas de São Francisco wine lodge (➤ 36–37).

SHOPS
Artecouro

Specializes in beautiful leather goods produced by local craftsmen (you can visit the factory at Rua Carlos Azevedo Menezes 16).

✉ Rua da Alfândega 15 ☎ 291 237 256 🕐 Mon–Fri 10–7, Sat 10–1

Artur de Barros e Sousa

Visitors are greeted by the warm evocative smells of old wood and rich wine at this old cobbled-floor wine lodge.

✉ Rua dos Ferreiros 109, Funchal ☎ 291 220 622 🕐 Mon–Fri 10–7, Sat 10–1

Bazar Oliveiras

Everything from honey cake *(bolo de mel)* to videos of Madeira, and from tacky keyrings to sophisticated handmade embroidery.

✉ Rua das Murcas 6 ☎ 291 224 632 🕐 Daily 10–7

Jose Carlos de Sousa

Handmade traditional leather ankle boots for men and women, plus comfortable sandals. Also sold in Funchal's Mercado dos Lavradores (➤ 42–43).

✉ Rua do Portão de São Tiago 22 (Zona Velha) ☎ 291 934 663 🕐 Mon–Fri 10–7, Sat 10–1

Patricio & Gouveia

One of the best and biggest factories in Madeira, with a large selection of garments and table linen.

✉ Rua do Visconde de Anadia 33 ☎ 291 220 801 🕐 Mon–Fri 10–7, Sat 10–1

Sports

DIVING
Manta Diving Centre
One of several long-established diving clubs offering a
beginners course leading to the CMAS Bronze qualification,
and a varied programme of dives at sites around the island.
✉ Galo Resort Hotel, Caniço de Baixo ☎ 291 935 588;
www.mantadiving.com

FISHING
Big Game Fishing
One of several charter boats for rent around Funchal
Marina, fully equipped and crewed for bottom fishing or big
game fishing. All fish are released once caught and tagged.
✉ Funchal Marina ☎ 291 934 996; www.biggamecharters.com

GOLF
See page 67.

HEALTH AND FITNESS
If you want a holiday specifically for this purpose,
investigate the Choupana Hills Resort (☎ 291 206 020),
which specializes in health and beauty therapies, or the Jardim do
Atlântico (➤ 76), which offers yoga, meditation and dance classes.

HORSE-BACK RIDING
Club Ipismo
Explore hidden parts of Madeira from the back of a horse (beginners
and experienced riders welcome). The mansion that houses the
stables is on the ER201 Terreiro da Luta road above Monte.
✉ Quinta Vale Pires, Caminho dos Pretos, Soã João Latrão ☎ 291 792 582

MOTORSPORTS
Madeira Wine Rally
The Madeira Wine Rally is regarded as one of the toughest stages

in the European rallying championship. It takes place during the first week in August. Visitors may find certain roads closed then, especially to the west of the island; the rally route centres around the flat Paul da Serra plateau between Funchal and Porto do Moniz. You can watch the start and finish of the daily stages in Avenida Arriaga, in central Funchal.

SWIMMING

Because Madeira lacks classic sand beaches, the luxury hotels of the hotel district have all invested in high-quality swimming facilities, most of which are open to non-residents for a small fee.

The biggest public pool complex is the Lido, on Rua Gorgulho, in the Hotel Zone (☎ 291 762 217). Further out of Funchal is the Clube Naval do Funchal (✉ Estrada Pontinha ☎ 291 762 253).

TENNIS AND SQUASH
Quinta do Magnólia

The elegant Quinta do Magnólia was built as the British Country Club but now belongs to the Madeiran regional government. The former clubhouse is now a public library. Pretty gardens surround it and, for those in search of exercise, there is a full range of sports facilities, including tennis courts, a large swimming pool, a putting course, squash courts and a jogging track. Entrance is free, and reservations to use the squash and tennis courts should be made at the gatekeeper's lodge at the entrance.

✉ Rua Dr Pita ☎ 291 764 598 🕓 Daily 7:30am–9pm

Entertainment and nightlife

CINEMA

Several of Madeira's new shopping centres (➤ 115–116) have multi-screen cinemas showing recently released films in their original language (with Portuguese subtitles). The most central is Cinemax in the Marina Shopping Centre on Avenida Arriaga. The Lusomondo is in the Forum Madeira shopping centre at the far western end of the Hotel Zone (Estrada Monumental 390), while further out is the Castello Lopez cinema in the Madeira Shopping Centre. Programmes start around 2pm and go on until late evening. Tickets go on sale an hour before each screening.

CLASSICAL MUSIC

Funchal has a thriving musical *conservatoire*, and you may be fortunate enough to catch a concert by students and teachers during your stay. Many of them are organized under the aegis of the Orquestra Clássica da Madeira (☎ 291 744 826). Ask at the Tourist Office for details of forthcoming events or look for posters around town.

FOLK DANCING AND MUSIC

Most hotels offer folk-dancing evenings, and you can enjoy the same spectacle if you dine in the seafood restaurants lining the Yachting Marina in Funchal. At the best shows, the dancers and musicians will explain the origins and history of their dances, instruments and costumes. There are numerous folk groups around the island who perform at local festivals.

HOTEL-BASED ENTERTAINMENT

All the major hotels in Funchal's Hotel Zone have entertainment programmes that are also open to non-residents. They range from the ubiquitous Madeiran folk-dancing evenings to themed nights featuring the food and music of, say, France, Spain or Brazil.

MADEIRAN DANCE

Madeira's traditional dance reflects the burdens of rural patterns of work. In the Carrier's Dance, the dancers bend beneath the weight of the imaginary stacks of sugar cane or baskets of bananas they carry along the island's steep paths. In the Heavy Dance, the rhythmic stamping of the dancers' feet reflects the custom of crushing grapes for wine with bare feet.

MADEIRAN MUSIC

Musical accompaniment to Madeiran dance is provided by an instrument similar to a ukulele, known as the *braguinha*. Rhythm is provided by wooden castanets, called *castanholes*, and a notched stick, called a *raspadeira*, played like a washboard.

THEATRE

Teatro Baltazar Dias (☎ 291 220 416 – information), also known as the Teatro Municipal, is the focal point for the island's artistic and cultural life. There is a regular programme of concerts, dance, theatre (usually in Portuguese) and art film. Look out for events advertised outside the theatre on Avenida Arriaga.

Places to stay

JARDIM DO ATLÂNTICO (€€€)

One of the few luxury hotels in the western part of Madeira, the Atlântico promotes itself as a health resort, with a range of programmes, such as yoga, meditation, massage, hydrotherapy and acupuncture, as well as fitness classes and countryside walks.

✉ Lomba da Rocha, Prazeres, Calheta ☎ 291 822 200; www.jardimatlantico.com

PESTANA CASINO PARK (€€€)

This is the closest of Madeira's five-star hotels to central Funchal. It is also Madeira's liveliest hotel for nightlife, with a top-class cabaret programme, regular discos and a casino on the grounds. Rooms are large and well equipped and there are good swimming and tennis facilities in the grounds.

✉ Rua Imperatriz Dona Amélia, Funchal ☎ 291 209 100; www.pestana.com

PORTO SANTO (€€€)

The beautiful gardens of this hotel merge imperceptibly with Porto Santo's golden beach. There are windsurfing boards and bicycles available, plus a mini golf course and tennis courts.

✉ Ribeiro Cochino, Campo de Baixo ☎ 291 980 140; www.hotelportosanto.com

POUSADA DOS VINHÁTICOS (€€)

This charming rural inn caters for walkers exploring the unspoiled woodland terrain in the spectacular Serra da Água Valley, south of the Encumeada pass. Facilities are simple but adequate.

✉ Serra da Água ☎ 291 775 936; www.pousadadosvinhaticos.com

❓ Reserve in advance

QUINTA SPLENDIDA (€€€)

The old pink-walled *quinta* now houses an excellent restaurant; the rooms are set around a courtyard, surrounded by tropical gardens.

✉ Sítio de Vargem, Caniço ☎ 291 930 400; www.quintasplendida.com

QUINTINHA SÃO JOÃO (€€€)

A truly enchanting small hotel with an excellent restaurant, bar, two swimming pools, fitness room, games room and modern spa.

✉ Rua da Levada de São João 4, 2.5km (1.5 miles) from central Funchal ☎ 291 740 920; www.quintinhasaojoao.com

REID'S PALACE (€€€)

Reid's is one of the world's best-known and prestigious hotels. For some, this elegant, understated hotel will be far too formal (most guests wear evening dress for dinner though it's not compulsory); for others it will be a welcome escape from the bustling world.

✉ Estrada Monumental 139 ☎ 291 717 171; www.reidspalace.com

ROCA MAR (€€€)

The Roca Mar has a spectacular location on the clifftops south of Caniço. The rocky cove at the foot of the cliffs has been converted into a lido, with swimming pools, sun terraces and a pier for access to the sheltered blue waters just offshore. There's a full range of evening entertainment and a regular shuttle bus service to Funchal.

✉ Caniço de Baixa ☎ 291 934 334; www.hotelrocamar.com

Exploring

Madeira has never quite lost its image of being an island retreat for those in delicate health, a place where the bankrupt old nobility of Europe could flee to escape their debts, or a retirement home for impoverished former colonial servants. Young travellers used to turn up their noses at the thought of a destination with no beaches, and no nightlife.

It is, however, one of Europe's most intriguing destinations. The island's mountainous volcanic landscape is carved into scores of deep valleys and ravines, clothed in the luxuriant vegetation that thrives in the frost-free climate. Hundreds of miles of footpaths run alongside the network of irrigation canals *(levadas)*, bringing water from the wet side of the island to the drier south. Easy to follow, these paths lead you deep into the rural heart of the island, where the way of life has hardly caught up with the industrial era.

Funchal

Funchal means 'fennel' and the city's name is said to derive from the abundance of fennel plants that Zarco, the island's discoverer, found growing here when he arrived in 1420.

High above the harbour, on the clifftops west of the city, is the Hotel Zone, where most visitors to Madeira stay. The area is almost a self-contained town, with its tourist shops and supermarkets, its lido complex and restaurants. Downtown Funchal is split into three sectors by its rivers, now enclosed between high embankments to prevent the flash floods that previously claimed several lives.

In the eastern sector of the city is the Zona Velha, or Old Town (➤ 54–55), with its many restaurants. The central sector contains a jumble of embroidery factories, crumbling town houses and shops selling pungent salt cod and dried herbs. Most of Funchal's cultural sights are packed into the maze of streets in the westernmost third of the city, focused around the Sé (➤ 52–53) and the Alfândega Velha (Old Customs House), now the Madeiran parliament building.

✚ 19M

ADEGAS DE SÃO FRANCISCO

Best places to see, ➤ 36–37.

CONVENTO DE SANTA CLARA

High walls surround the Convent of the Poor Clares, shutting off from the world Madeira's oldest religious foundation. Santa Clara was founded in 1496 by João Gonçalves de Câmara, one of the grandsons of Zarco, the discoverer of Madeira. Zarco's granddaughter, Dona Isabella, was installed as the first abbess, establishing a tradition of aristocratic patronage that ensured that the convent was richly endowed. Many a daughter of wealthy parents was forced to take the veil on reaching her eighteenth birthday, a practice that was supposed to confer spiritual benefits on both parents and child. The convent became a popular tourist attraction in the 19th century, when visitors would come ostensibly to buy flowers made of feathers and sample sweetmeats made by the nuns, but in reality hoping to catch sight of some legendary beauty, tragically cut off from the delights of the world.

Today the nuns run a well-regarded kindergarten. Ring the bell on the gate and you will be given a guided tour of the chapels that lie off the peaceful 15th-century cloisters. The chapels shelter an astonishing wealth of paintings, sculpture and *azulejos* tiles, and in due course these will be housed in a new museum. The church alongside is on the site of a 15th-century chapel where the island's first three governors, including Zarco, were buried. Glazed *azulejos* decorate the domed church tower, and there are more ancient tiles, faded but still impressive, covering the walls. Above is a typical Madeiran church ceiling of timber, painted with floral patterns and a galleon in full sail.

✚ *Funchal 1a* ✉ Calçada de Santa Clara ☎ 291 742 602 🕐 Mon–Sat 10–12, 3–5; Sun 10–12; ring for entry if door is closed, but not over the lunch period 🖐 Moderate

FORTALEZA DE SÃO TIAGO

Attracted by stories of Madeira's massive sugar-derived wealth, French, English, Algerian and Turkish pirates regularly attacked Funchal from the 16th century, looting churches and wine cellars and killing anyone who stood in their way. In response, Madeira's governor ordered the construction of massive walls and fortifications, which were extended and reinforced over a 100-year period. Built in 1614, the Fortress of St James was one of the last fortifications to be completed. It is also the only fort fully open to the public, since the others are still used by the Portuguese military. Newly restored, the building now houses a museum of contemporary art, but the rather unexciting works on display are a distraction from the real interest of the fortress – the maze of passages, staircases and towers, which make a perfect playground for children, and the views over the rooftops of Funchal to be had from the ramparts.

✚ *Funchal 6c* ✉ Rua do Portão de São Tiago ☎ 291 213 340 🕐 Mon–Sat 10–12:30, 2–5:30. Closed Sun, public hols 🖐 Moderate 🍴 Restaurant (€€); eat lunch here and admission to the fortress is free

IBTAM HANDICRAFTS INSTITUTE

IBTAM is the body that oversees standards in Madeira's economically important embroidery industry, and the small museum on the first floor of its headquarters building is a showcase for Madeiran handicrafts. The rather drab and old-fashioned displays are brought to life by the vibrant colours of traditional island costume, including scarlet and yellow skirts, waistcoats and scarves. Also on display are intricately embroidered tablecloths and bedspreads, and diaphanous nightgowns. On the staircase leading up to the museum is an impressive tapestry depicting a flower-filled Madeiran landscape, made in 1958–61 and comprising some 7 million stitches.

✚ *Funchal 5a* ✉ Rua do Visconde de Anadia 44 ☎ 291 223 141
🕐 Mon–Fri 10–12:30, 2:30–5:30. Closed Sat, Sun, public hols ✋ Moderate

JARDIM BOTÂNICO

Nineteenth-century writers bestowed many fanciful names on Madeira to describe the island's botanical wealth – 'a floating greenhouse' and 'God's botanical garden' being among them. The first plant seeds were probably carried by oceanic currents from West Africa, or reached Madeira in bird droppings. Thriving in the island's fertile volcanic soil, species evolved that are unique to the island. Early settlers may have destroyed many more plants as they slashed and burned the island's dense vegetation. Zarco ordered the island's woods to be set alight, and such was the ferocity of the resulting blaze that the explorers were driven back to their ships, eventually being forced to put out to sea to escape the heat.

Even so, it is unlikely that the whole island was burned, for several large areas of wilderness remain on Madeira, and the Botanical Garden displays examples of the kind of trees and shrubs that make up Madeira's virgin forest. Among them is the dragon tree, with its smooth bark and claw-like leaf clusters, valued since ancient times for its red sap used for cloth dyeing.

Competing with the dragon tree are the many strange and colourful plants introduced to Madeira from far-distant lands, all displayed here in a series of terraced beds. Stars of the show include the tropical orchids (in flower from November to March), while other beds are devoted to the plants that underpin Madeira's cut-flower trade – such as bird of paradise plants and arum lilies – and a fine collection of cacti and sculptural agaves.

➕ *Funchal 5a (off map)*/19L ✉ Quinta do Bom Sucesso, Caminho do Meio ☎ 291 211 200 🕐 Daily 9–5:30. Closed public hols ✋ Moderate (includes entrance to nearby Jardim dos Loiros; ► below) 🍴 Café (€) in grounds 🚌 Town bus 31 or cable car from Monte

JARDIM DOS LOIROS

Exotic screeches, whoops and squawks advertise the presence of this tropical bird garden, where even the brightest flowers are put in the shade by the plumage of cockatoos, parrots and macaws.

Children will enjoy the antics of the birds, which are displayed in aviaries dotted around the gardens.

➕ *Funchal 5a (off map)*/19L ✉ Caminho do Meio ☎ 291 211 200 🕐 Daily 9–5:30. Closed public hols ✋ Moderate (includes entrance to nearby Jardim Botânico; ► above) 🚌 Town bus 31 or cable car from Monte

JARDIM DE SANTA CATARINA

This public park is named after the Chapel of St Catherine, founded in 1425 by Constança Rodriguez, wife of Zarco. The little chapel, with its attractive porch and holy water stoup, stands on a terrace from which there are good views of the harbour.

Elsewhere the park is dotted with sculptures, ranging from a modernist fountain featuring a female torso to the vigorous bronze figure of the Semeador, the Sower (1919), by Francisco Franco. The Sower metaphorically broadcasts his seed across immaculate flower beds, and the upper part of the garden, with its aviaries and children's playground, has many fine tropical flowering trees. From the park, you can walk uphill into the well-tended and shady grounds of the Quinta Vigia, the pink-painted mansion that forms the official residence of Madeira's president. On the opposite side of the road is the Hospicio da Princesa, built as a tuberculosis sanatorium in 1859, with another fine garden featuring several ancient dragon trees.

✚ *Funchal 1d* ✉ Avenida do Infante ⏰ 24 hours ✋ Free 🍴 Café (€) in grounds

MADEIRA STORY CENTRE

The Madeira Story Centre, in the Old Town (Zona Velha), is a great place to go early in your visit to Madeira for an overview of the island's history. The exhibits appeal to children as well as adults, with touch-screen interactive quizzes, ferocious French pirates and even a few smells. Crammed into the main exhibition area are maps, astrolabes and models of the ships that carried early settlers from Portugal to Madeira, a working model of a sugar mill and screens showing Pathé News film footage from the 1950s

and 1960s. A mock-up of an Aquila Airways airline cabin hints at the luxury enjoyed by passengers on seaplane flights between Southampton and Funchal from 1949 to 1958, with Winston Churchill, and Gregory Peck (star of *Moby Dick*, filmed in Madeira in 1956) among the passengers.

✚ *Funchal 5c* ✉ Rua Dom Carlos I 27–29 ☎ 291 000 770; www.storycentre.com 🕐 Daily 10–6. Closed 25 Dec ✋ Expensive

MERCADO DOS LAVRADORES

Best places to see, ➤ 42–43.

MUSEU 'A CIDADE DO AÇÚCAR'

This history museum has been erected around the excavated remains of a house built in 1495 for Jeanin Esmerandt, a Flemish merchant working for the Bruges-based Company Despars. The significance of the house is that Christopher Columbus twice stayed here as a guest of Esmerandt: once in 1480, and again in 1498 (after his pioneering voyage across the Atlantic to the Americas) when he stayed for six days. The original house was demolished in 1876 and excavated in 1989. Finds from the excavation exhibited here include pottery, food remains (nuts, seashells and animal bones), jewellery, coins and bone buttons. Also on display here are ceramic sugar cones, similar to those which feature on Funchal's coat of arms, and 16th-century engravings of the sugar-making process. The enormous wealth that sugar brought to Funchal is represented here by religious paintings and statues acquired by the city's merchants.

✚ *Funchal 3c* ✉ Praça do Colombo ☎ 291 236 910 🕐 Mon–Fri 10–12:30, 2–6. Closed Sat, Sun, public hols ✋ Moderate 🍴 Cafés (€) in nearby Largo da Sé (cathedral square)

MUSEU DE ARTE SACRA

Best places to see, ➤ 46–47.

MUSEU FRANCO

This quiet and little-visited museum celebrates the artistic achievements of two brothers born on Madeira but who achieved fame on the wider European stage. Henrique Franco (1883–1961) was a painter and his older brother Francisco (1855–1955) was a sculptor. Both studied in Paris, where they were friendly with Picasso, Degas and Modigliani, but their careers were largely centred on the Portuguese capital, Lisbon.

The first part of the museum is devoted to a series of Gauginesque portraits, painted by Henrique. He often painted his subjects – from weather-beaten peasants to industrialists and aristocrats – against a colourful background of flowers and foliage reminiscent of the Madeiran landscape.

Francisco's vigorous but monochrome sculptures in the second part of the museum are evidence of a busy life devoted to designing public memorials, coins, medals and postage stamps, including such sculptures as the Zarco monument in central Funchal and the *Semeador* in the Jardim de Santa Catarina (➤ 88).

✚ *Funchal 4a* ✉ Rua João de Deus 13
☎ 291 230 633 🕐 Mon–Fri 10–12:30, 2–6. Closed Sat, Sun, public hols ✋ Moderate
🍴 Pavement cafés and coffee bars abound in Praça do Carmo, off Rua das Hortas (two blocks south of the museum)

MUSEU FREITAS

Halfway up the steep and cobbled Calçada de Santa Clara is this balconied town house, whose stately rooms provide a glimpse of life on Madeira at any time over the last 150 years.

The first part of the museum consists of a gallery covering the history of *azulejos* tiles, those brightly coloured ceramics that decorate church walls all over Madeira, as well as domestic homes. Originating in the Islamic east, the practice of using tiles spread from Persia to Portugal via Moorish North Africa and Spain. Madeira lacked suitable clays to produce its own tiles so imported them from Seville in the 16th century, then from the Netherlands. Examples of tiles from Santa Clara convent are among the earliest exhibits, while the last flowering of tile manufacture includes some lovely art nouveau ones.

The second part of the museum consists of the house bequeathed to Funchal by Dr Frederico de Freitas, in 1978. It dates back to the late 17th century. A conservatory in the garden, a glass-roofed winter garden and art nouveau furnishing all lend charm to a house crammed with fascinating objects collected by Dr Freitas during his world travels. The collections include oriental carpets, religious paintings, *azulejos* and fine antique furnishings, as well as

17th- and 18th-century hand-carved crib figures originating from mainland Portugal and the Portuguese colonies of Goa and Macau.
✚ *Funchal 1b* ✉ Calçada de Santa Clara 7 ☎ 291 220 578 ⏰ Tue–Sat 10–12:30, 2–5:30, Sun 10–12:30. Closed Mon, public hols ✋ Moderate

MUSEU MUNICIPAL

The Municipal Museum has a tiny aquarium on the ground floor stocked with the fish that are typically caught off Madeiran shores, including grouper fish, moray eels and bottom-dwelling flounders. Upstairs is a collection of stuffed birds and animals, including sharks with gaping jaws and giant crabs with metre-long claws. Displays of Madeiran birds are as close as you are likely to get to the more elusive species that nest on inaccessible cliffs.
✚ *Funchal 1b* ✉ Rua da Mouraria 31 ☎ 291 229 761 ⏰ Tue–Fri 10–6, Sat, Sun, public hols 12–6. Closed Mon, 25 Dec, 1 Jan ✋ Moderate

a walk exploring Funchal's architecture

Discover Funchal's rich architectural heritage on a stroll through the city centre.

Start at the Câmara Municipal (Town Hall).

The elegant 18th-century mansion was built for the Count of Carvalhal but sold by his profligate heirs. The delightful palm-filled courtyard features a graceful sculpture of *Leda and the Swan* (1880). Turn your back on the entrance to view Praça do Município (Town Square), paved with grey basalt and white marble in a fish-scale pattern. To the right, gesticulating saints decorate the facade of the Igreja di Colégio, the Jesuit church, founded in 1574. To the left is the Bishop's Palace of 1600, now housing the Museu de Arte Sacra (Sacred Art Museum ➤ 46–47).

Cross the square, heading for the far right-hand corner. Walk up shop-lined Rua C Pestana and carry straight on at the next junction, along traffic-free Rua da Carreira.

Three doors up on the left, in Rua da Carreira, is the entrance to The Pátio complex, with its courtyard café and Vicentes photographic museum (➤ 98–99). Try coffee here, or buy typical Madeiran *bolo de mel* (literally 'honey cake' but actually made with molasses) at the baker's further up on the left.

Walk up Rua da Carreira.

As you dip in and out of the street's characterful shops, look up to see the pretty wrought-iron balconies that decorate many of the upper storeys. Among the best houses is No 155.

The third turn right (Rua do Quobra Costas) leads to the English Church (completed 1822), set in a pretty garden.

At the end of Rua da Carreira is the British Cemetery (Cimitero Inglesa), the burial ground of Madeira's Protestants of all nationalities, worth visiting for its many poignant 19th-century memorials and epitaphs.

Distance 1km (half a mile)
Time 30 minutes
Start point Câmara Municipal (Town Hall), Praça do Município
➕ Funchal 3b
End point British Cemetery, Rua da Carreira. To enter the cemetery, ring the bell at No 235
Lunch O Pátio Café (€) ✉ Rua da Carreira 43 ☎ 291 227 376

O PÁTIO

O Pátio (The Patio) is a charming building dating from the 1860s, consisting of a courtyard and café, open to the sky, shaded by palms and surrounded by an arcade of small shops. Rising from the cobbled court-yard is an ornate double staircase with wrought-iron balustrades, leading up to a fanciful balcony of similar design, looking like a saloon bar in some Wild West movie.

The upper floor houses the photo-graphic studio of Vicente Gomes da Silva, founded in 1865, when the art of photography was still relatively new. In fact, this was the first commercial photographic studio to be established in Portugal; such was the demand for holiday souvenirs from wealthy visitors to Madeira that Gomes da Silva felt confident in pouring a small fortune into the purchase of mahogany and brass-bound plate cameras, together with all the paraphernalia of the darkroom. Visitors to the studio can browse through a selection of the 380,000 or so photographs that have survived in the Vicentes collection, a rich resource covering nearly 140 years of island history, and look at a collection of antique cameras, costumes and studio props.

✚ *Funchal 2b* ✉ Rua da Carreira 43 ☎ 291 225 050 (museum); 291 227 376 (café) 🕐 O Patio: daily 9–6. Museum: Tue–Sat 10–12:30, 2–5. Closed Sun, Mon and public hols

PICO (CASTELO DO PICO)

It is a sweaty, heart-pounding climb up to the Pico, or Radio Peak as it is known locally because of the naval communications masts bristling from its heights. It is worth the effort for the *castelo*, built in 1632–40 to warn of sea attack. A walk around the walls is rewarding for the views down across Funchal's rooftops and up to the wooded heights above the city. A small exhibition room in the castle traces its history through old engravings.

✚ *Funchal 1a (off map)/*19M ✉ Rua do Castelo 🕐 Daily 9–6 🖐 Free

QUINTA DAS CRUZES

Of the many fine mansions built by wealthy merchants around Funchal, the Quinta das Cruzes (the Mansion of the Crosses) is the only one open to the public. Zarco, the discoverer of Madeira and the island's first governor, built his house on this site in the 1450s, but little remains from this era except for some architectural fragments displayed in the gardens. These include gravestones, crosses and broken pieces of church fonts, as well as all that remains of Funchal's pillory, where miscreants were once publicly flogged. Most striking of all are two stone window frames, carved with dancing figures and man-eating lions in the style known as Manueline, after the reigning monarch.

The present house dates from the 17th century, when it was built for the Lomelino family, wealthy wine merchants from Genova. Furnished in the Empire style, which was popular at the time, the rooms are arranged thematically, with sections devoted to oriental art, French porcelain, topographical views and portraits, costume and crib figures.

The basement contains an unusual collection of furniture made from recycled packing cases. Sugar was once so precious that it was shipped in chests made from best Brazilian satinwood. Once competition from the New World destroyed Madeira's sugar trade, enterprising cabinetmakers reused the wood to make the fine cupboards displayed here.

✛ *Funchal 1a* ✉ Calçada do Pico 1 ☎ 291 740 670 🕓 Tue–Sat 10–12:30, 2–5:30, Sun 10–1. Closed Mon, public hols ✋ Moderate

SÉ (CATHEDRAL)

Best places to see, ➤ 52–53.

ZONA VELHA (OLD TOWN)

Best places to see, ➤ 54–55.

HOTELS

Apartamento da Sé (€)

This new apartment block offers stylish double rooms and studios at bargain rates right in the heart of the city, a block south of the cathedral (Sé).

✉ Rua do Sabão 53 ☎ 291 214 600

Apartamentos Avenue Park (€€)

Opposite the Casino on the main Avenida do Infante, these are centrally located self-catering apartments, each with kitchen, living room, bathroom and bedroom, plus parking in the basement: perfect for independent travellers who don't want hotel facilities. The rooms are well soundproofed, but the sunny south-facing balconies front a busy road.

✉ Avenida do Infante 26 ☎ 291 242 712; www.avenuepark-madeira.com

Choupana Hills Resort (€€€)

The Choupana is inspired by Balinese architecture, with accommodation in timber cabins set in beautifully landscaped grounds high above Funchal. Excellent spa facilities and a first-class restaurant make this a pleasure-seeker's paradise.

✉ Travessa do Largo da Choupana ☎ 291 206 020; www.choupanahills.com

Crowne Plaza (€€€)

The stunning design of this stylish hotel – with its Phillipe Starck furniture and wave-shaped roofline – is matched by luxurious rooms, fine dining and polished service, plus full resort facilities.

✉ Estrada Monumental 175–177 ☎ 291 717 700; www.crowneplaza.com

Eden Mar (€€)

Excellent value aparthotel close to the supermarkets and the Lido complex in the Hotel Zone. The studios and suites all have a kitchenette with fridge and two cooking rings. Facilities on site include a swimming pool, gym, sauna, Jacuzzi and tennis courts.

✉ Rua do Gorgulho 2 ☎ 291 709 700; www.edenmar.com

Pestana Carlton (€€€)

Along with the Savoy and the Pestana Casino Park, the Pestana Carlton Madeira enjoys a location close to downtown Funchal. The hotel is in two parts; rooms in the 16-storey main block enjoy fine views to the harbour or the mountains, while the pool terrace block has rooms looking over the hotel's two large swimming pools. For children there is a play area, and a Kids' Activity Club operates during the summer.

✉ Largo António Nobre ☎ 291 239 500; www.pestana.com

Pestana Casino Park (€€€)

See page 76.

Porto Santa Maria (€€)

This smart hotel in the Zona Velha brings luxury to a part of Funchal that has only had inexpensive, old-fashioned accommodation up to now. The hotel is perfectly located for visitors who want to be right where the action is, without sacrificing the facilities of a trendy hotel. The hotel is fronted by a sun terrace with outdoor pool and bar.

✉ 20 Avenida do Mar ☎ 291 206 700; www.portobay.com

Quinta da Bela Vista (€€€)

It's a stiff walk up to this elegant mansion hotel (some 15 minutes from the centre), but the price is worth paying for stylishly furnished rooms, many with antiques, and lovely gardens.

✉ Caminho Avista Navios 4 ☎ 291 706 400; www.belavistamadeira.com

Quinta da Penha de França (€€)

Many *quintas* (aristocratic mansions) were swept away when Funchal's Hotel Zone was created in the 1980s, but this fine building managed to survive in a prime spot behind the Pestana Casino Park hotel. Now converted to a fine hotel itself, the *quinta* is a place of old-fashioned elegance combined with all mod cons.

✉ Rua Imperatrice Dona Amélia 83 ☎ 291 775 936; www.penhafranca.com

Quinta das Vistas (€€€)

The Mansion of the Views could not be better named, with its terraces offering panoramic views over Funchal's rooftops. Palm-fringed public areas and deluxe bedrooms provide a fleeting taste of a charmed lifestyle.

✉ Caminho de Santo António 52 ☎ 291 775 936; www.quintadasvistasmadeira.com

Quinta de Casa Branca (€€€)

Modernist architecture at its best (the work of local architect João Favila) ensures that this cleverly disguised accommodation sits well within the hotels' lush tropical garden setting, with each room opening out onto green lawns and flower-filled borders, while the original old house serves as the restaurant.

✉ Rua da Casa Branca 9 ☎ 291 700 770; www.quintacasabranca.pt

Quinta do Sol (€€)

This friendly hotel overlooks the gardens of the Quinta do Magnólia park, with its tennis and squash courts, which guests can use for a small charge. In addition, the hotel has its own heated swimming pool and games room. For an added touch of luxury, go for rooms in the new wing. The hotel puts on a weekly folk show, plus live music most nights in the cocktail bar.

✉ Rua Dr Pita 6 ☎ 291 707 010

Quinta Perestrello (€€)

This small 19th-century mansion has rooms in a modern wing. Those at the front suffer from traffic noise so if that bothers you, be sure to secure a room overlooking the gardens at the rear.

✉ Rua do Dr Pita 3 ☎ 291 775 936; www.quintaperestrellomadeira.com

Quintinha São João (€€€)

See page 77.

Reid's Palace (€€€)

See page 77.

Residencial Gordon (€)

Caught in a time warp, the Gordon is a quiet, old-fashioned hotel. Some rooms overlook the pretty gardens of the English Church (whose library is open to visitors; the coffee mornings that take place here after the Sunday morning service also provide a popular meeting point for visitors and long-stay Madeira residents).

✉ Rua do Quebra Costas 34 ☎ 291 742 366

Residencial Santa Clara (€)

The Santa Clara hotel offers budget accommodation in a gracious and dignified old building with grand interiors. The catch is that it is a stiff uphill walk from the centre of Funchal, past the Santa Clara Convent, so you need to be fit to get here.

✉ Calçada do Pico 16B ☎ 291 742 194

Savoy Resort (€€€)

The Savoy is quiet and dignified, but also caters for families, with friendly staff and an excellent range of sports facilities. There is a choice of rooms in the older Classic Savoy or the more luxurious Royal Savoy, on the seafront. Both share the leisure complex.

✉ Avenida do Infante ☎ 291 213 000; www.savoyresort.com

White Waters (€€)

A family-run, 3-star hotel in the very heart of Machico that is traditional and contemporary all at the same time. It is close to the town centre, coffee shops, restaurants and bars.

✉ Presceta 25 de Abril, Machico ☎ 291 969 380; www.whitewaters-madeira.com

Windsor (€)

This friendly modern hotel is buried in the heart of the maze of lanes near the Carmo church in central Funchal. Most rooms face into an inner courtyard, rather than onto the street, so noise is not a problem. There is a tiny rooftop pool, and ample parking in the hotel garage.

✉ Rua das Hortas 4C ☎ 291 233 081; www.hotelwindsorgroup.pt

RESTAURANTS

A Muralha (€€)

As well as all the usual Madeiran specialities, A Muralha serves several more unusual regional dishes, including *picadinho* (fragrant herby stewed beef) and wild rabbit.

✉ Largo do Corpo Santo 2 ☎ 291 232 561 🕐 Lunch, dinner

A Rampa (€€)

Located opposite the Savoy Hotel, A Rampa is a favourite with families, serving authentic pizzas and pasta dishes, including children's favourites such as macaroni and spaghetti Bolognese, as well as fresh salads and more substantial fish and meat dishes, cooked in the Italian style. Friendly waiters and good-value prices.

✉ Henry II Building 1st Floor, Avenida do Infante ☎ 291 235 275
🕐 Lunch, dinner

Armazém do Sal (€€)

Located in an old salt warehouse in the centre of Funchal, this restaurant is well worth a visit. Superb Madeiran cuisine with a twist and an excellent wine list.

✉ Rua da Alfândega 135 ☎ 291 241 285 🕐 Lunch, dinner Mon–Fri, dinner Sat. Closed Sun

Arsénio's (€€)

See page 58.

Bombay Palace (€€)

This excellent tandoori restaurant makes a welcome change from Madeiran sardines, kebabs and tuna. Try the tandoori fishr.

✉ Eden Mar Shopping Centre, Rua do Gorgulho ☎ 291 763 110 🕐 Lunch, dinner

Brasserie (€€€)

Breaking free of the traditional Madeiran mould, Brasserie offers modern cooking and a stylish setting for a special meal of fish, game, lamb, beef or even venison.

✉ Promenade do Lido ☎ 291 763 325 🕐 Dinner

Casal da Penha (€€)

Pretty dining room and good choice of fish and salads, plus large rooftop terrace with views over gardens to the sea.

✉ Rua Penha de França 1 ☎ 291 227 674 🕐 Lunch, dinner

Casa Velha (€€€)

Ideal for a special night out, set in a villa with flower-filled gardens. Specializes in *flambé* dishes and lobster.

✉ Rua Imperatriz Dona Amélia 69 ☎ 291 205 600 🕐 Lunch, dinner

Don Filet (€€)

Beef is king at this restaurant, where you can eat your fillets Brazilian style, broiled over a charcoal grill, or Madeiran style, skewered on a bay twig and flavoured with garlic.

✉ Rua do Favilla 7 ☎ 291 764 426 🕐 Lunch, dinner. Closed Sun lunch

Dona Amélia (€€)

An elegant and well-restored town house with a terrace garden makes an atmospheric setting for the international-style cuisine served here.

✉ Rua Imperatriz Dona Amélia 83 ☎ 291 225 784 🕐 Lunch, dinner

Fleur de Lys (€€€)

For not much more than the cost of a meal in some of Funchal's downtown restaurants, you can treat yourself to the sophisticated ambience of the Savoy Hotel's flagship restaurant, while enjoying great views over Funchal and the harbour. Reservations are essential. Dress code.

✉ Savoy Resort, Avenida do Infante ☎ 291 213 000 🕐 Dinner

Fora d'Água (€€)

Adventurous partnerings of traditional Madeiran food with non-traditional garnishes and flavourings, such as parrot fish with ginger, garlic and celery purée or prawns with pineapple and lemon marmalade.

✉ Promenade do Lido (below Tivoli Ocean Park Hotel)
☎ 291 764 192 🕐 Dinner

Gavião Novo (€€)

Busy restaurant that fills up quickly, in the Old Town, specializing in fish. It is always worth asking the waiters what is best because they often have specials not listed on the main menu – it all depends what the fishermen who supply them manage to hook.

✉ Rua Santa Maria 131 ☎ 291 229 238 🕐 Lunch, dinner

Glória Latina (€€)

Popular late-night haunt (open until 2am) with a cocktail bar, terrace restaurant and live Brazilian-style music.

✉ Rua Imperatriz Dona Amélia 101 ☎ 291 282 266 🕐 Lunch, dinner (high season only)

Golden Gate (€)

See page 58.

Kon Tiki (€€)

After a week of meat kebabs and *espada* (scabbard fish), visitors seeking a change could do worse than visit the Kon Tiki restaurant for beef broiled on hot lava stones (Finnish style) or shark steak. Inevitably, *espada* is on offer too, but here the flamboyant waiters *flambé* the fish at your table with prawns.

✉ Rua do Favilla 9 ☎ 291 764 737 🕐 Lunch, dinner

Le Jardin (€€)

French influences are to be found in the cooking at this Old Town restaurant specializing in *flambé* fish and peppered steak.

✉ Rua de Carlos I 60 ☎ 291 222 864 🕐 Lunch, dinner

Les Faunes (€€€)

Arguably Madeira's most romantic restaurant, and the place to eat if expense is no object, serving top-quality French cuisine. The airy dining room is decorated with Picasso drawings of fauns. In summer the restaurant transforms itself into the 'Brisa do Mar' al fresco restaurant and moves to the outdoor terrace. Dress smartly. Reservations advised.

✉ Reid's Hotel, Estrada Monumental ☎ 291 717 171 🕐 Dinner. Closed Mon

Londres (€€)

Despite the name, Londres specializes in mainland Portuguese dishes, including *bacalhau* (salt cod) for which there are said to be as many recipes as there are days in the year. They serve a different Portuguese speciality every day, but fresh fish is always available.

✉ Rua da Carreira 64A ☎ 291 235 329 🕐 Lunch, dinner. Closed Sun

Mar Azul (€€)

Do not be put off by the sight of keen waiters outside touting for business, possibly implying that this is a tourist rip-off joint. The food is excellent, as is the entertainment – Madeiran folk dancers perform authentic island dances on the pavement outside and even those who hate the idea of 'folk' will be charmed. Prices are reasonable so long as you avoid the lobster.

✉ Funchal Yacht Marina, Avenida das Comunidades Madeirenses ☎ 291 230 079 🕐 Lunch, dinner

Marina Terrace (€€)

Another waterside restaurant located on the northern rim of the Yacht Marina, serving everything from pizza to lobster. Staff are in Madeiran costume and there is live folk dancing in the main season.

✉ Marina do Funchal ☎ 291 230 547 🕐 Lunch, dinner

Marisa (€€)

When you visit this tiny Old Town restaurant you feel as if you are a guest in someone's home, as father and son cook delicious seafood and rice dishes while mother takes the orders and waits at table. Very good value.

✉ Rua de Santa Maria 162 ☎ 291 226 189 🕐 Lunch, dinner

Moby Dick (€€)

Fish restaurant in the Hotel Zone serving a wide range of fresh fish, from *espada de camarão* (scabbard fish with prawns) to *atum con todos* (tuna with everything!).

✉ Estrada Monumental 187 ☎ 291 776 868 🕐 Lunch, dinner; closed Sun

O Almirante (€€)

Walls decorated with nautical memorabilia and paintings of ships set the theme for this popular Old Town restaurant specializing in meat on the spit, fish and shellfish.

✉ Largo do Poço 1–2 ☎ 291 224 252 🕐 Lunch, dinner

O Barquiero (€€)

Fish and seafood in a bewildering variety but all fresh and tasty in this popular restaurant on the cliffs at the east end of the beach at Praia Formosa.

✉ Centro Comercial Centromar, Rua Ponta da Cruz (far western end of the Estrada Monumental) ☎ 291 761 229 🕐 Lunch, dinner

O Celeiro (€€)

The intimate Cellar restaurant is a good place to sample *caldeirada* (fish casserole) or the southern Portuguese speciality of *cataplana de mariscos* (seafood casserole).

✉ Rua dos Aranhas 22 ☎ 291 230 622 🕐 Lunch, dinner

O Jango (€€)

This intimate Old Town restaurant, converted from a former fisherman's home, specializes in seafood. Fans return again and again for the *cataplana*, a hearty fish stew whose ingredients are never the same two days running – the contents depending on what the local fishermen who supply the restaurant have caught that day. Excellent atmosphere.

✉ Rua de Santa Maria 166 ☎ 291 221 280 🕐 Lunch, dinner; closed 1–21 Jul

O Panorâmico (€€€)

If you like music with your meal, this is the place to come. The flagship restaurant at the Pestana Carlton Park Hotel offers dinner dances and live entertainment every Sunday, Monday, Tuesday and Thursday.

✉ Pestana Carlton Park, Largo António Nobre ☎ 291 209 100 🕐 Dinner

O Tapassol (€€)

A favourite of old Madeira hands, this Old Town restaurant has a tiny rooftop terrace and a menu featuring more unusual dishes, such as wild rabbit in season and octopus casserole.

✉ Rua Dom Carlos I 62 ☎ 291 225 023 🕔 Lunch, dinner

Portão (€€)

In a sheltered corner to the rear of the Corpo Santo chapel in the Old Town, Portão is a quieter and more intimate restaurant than those on the main drag. Choose between authentic Portuguese salt cod with boiled egg (a bras) or push the boat out with grilled lobster or prawns in champagne sauce – but save space for delicious Zabaionne Madeira, the classic Italian dessert made with Madeira rather than Marsala.

✉ Rua Portão de São Tiago 1 ☎ 291 221 125 🕔 Lunch, dinner

Prince Albert (€€)

Themed as a Victorian pub, with dark wood panelling and much cut glass, the Prince Albert tends to attract a mainly British crowd who enjoy the bonhomie of pub conversation. The dining room serves a range of good Portuguese and international food.

✉ Rua Imperatriz Dona Amélia 86 ☎ 291 235 793 🕔 Lunch, dinner

Quinta Palmeira (€€€)

This 19th-century quinta is a rare survivor of the elegant mansions that lined Avenida do Infante before the high-rise hotel blocks arrived. Eat in the elegant, mirrored dining room, or on the garden terrace, and choose from an extensive menu which includes several vegetarian dishes.

✉ Avenida do Infante 17–19 ☎ 291 221 814 🕔 Lunch, dinner

Riso (€€)

Serves a selection of rice dishes from around the world.

✉ Rua de Santa Maria 274 ☎ 291 280 360 🕔 Lunch, dinner

Vagrant (€€)

See page 59.

SHOPPING

BOOKS
Livraria Esperança
This wonderfully old-fashioned bookshop with branches on both sides of the street has a good selection of history books and academic texts for those who want to delve deep into Madeira's history.

✉ Rua dos Ferreiros 119 ☎ 291 221 116 🕓 Mon–Fri 10–6, Sat 10–1

COLLECTABLES
The Collectors Shop
Old postcards of Madeira make an unusual souvenir; browse for postcards, greetings cards, postage stamps, coins and banknotes, medallions and old book covers, as well as minerals and precious stones at this collectors' cornucopia.

✉ Avenida Arriaga 75 ☎ 291 223 070 🕓 Mon–Fri 10–7, Sat 10–1

EMBROIDERY AND TAPESTRY
Madeira Sun
Do-it-yourself tapestry kits at a fraction of the price you would pay for the finished articles.

✉ Avenida Zarco 4 🕓 Mon–Fri 10–7, Sat 10–1

Patricio & Gouveia
See page 71.

FLOWERS
You can buy flowers in the market or from stallholders around the cathedral square in Funchal, but the advantage of buying from shops is that they will pack your purchases in special protective boxes so that they will withstand the journey home.

A Rosa
Order your flowers two or three days before your departure and they will be delivered to your hotel fresh on the day you leave.

✉ Rua Imperatriz Dona Amélia 126 ☎ 291 764 111 🕓 Mon–Fri 10–7, Sat 10–1

Boa Vista Orchids

Whether you want to buy orchids or not, it is worth visiting Boa
Vista Orchids just for the lovely subtropical gardens that surround
the Quinta da Boa Vista (the well-named Good View Mansion).
✉ Rua Lombo da Boa Vista ☎ 291 220 468 🕐 Mon–Sat 9–5:30

Jardim Orquídea

The Orchid Garden is a working nursery with some 4,000 different
varieties of tropical orchid on display (flowering all year – main
season November to February). You can visit the breeding
laboratories and buy *in vitro* plants, grown in gel in a plastic tube to
take home (EU customs regulations allow the importation of plants
so long as there is no soil with them). Entrance charge.
✉ Garden: Rua Pita da Silva 37 ☎ 291 238 444 🕐 Daily 9–6
✉ Shop: Marina Shopping Centre Shop 202, Avenida Arriaga
🕐 Mon–Sat 11–7

Magnolia Flower Shop

Excellent selection of cut and dried flowers, plus pot plants, bulbs
and orchids.
✉ Loja 1, Casino Park Hotel Gardens ☎ 291 222 577 🕐 Daily 10–7

FURNISHINGS

Cayres

Cayres stocks a good selection of modern Portuguese ceramics.
✉ Rua Dr Fernão Ornelas 56A/B ☎ 291 226 104 🕐 Mon–Fri 10–7, Sat
10–11

Cookshop

If Portuguese ceramics are not your style, try this shop for chic
international tableware, from cocktail glasses and champagne
flutes to espresso machines.
✉ Galerias São Laurenço ☎ 291 227 050 🕐 Mon–Fri 10–7, Sat 10–5

Intemporâneo Interiores

Modern furniture, lighting and furnishing fabrics.
✉ Rua das Netos 18 ☎ 291 238 076 🕐 Mon–Fri 10–1, 3–7, Sat 10–1

Tribo

As its name suggests, this interior design shop stocks contemporary furnishings with an ethnic/tribal look.

✉ Arcadas de São Francisco 5 ☎ 291 236 222 🕐 Mon–Fri 10–7, Sat 10–5

LEATHERWORK

Artecouro

See page 71.

Safa Pele

A good choice of elegant leather handbags, wallets, briefcases and luggage.

✉ Rua das Murcas 26A ☎ 291 223 619 🕐 Daily 10–7

MARKETS

Although supermarkets exist on Madeira, many people still shop in the local covered market. There is a huge market – the Mercado dos Lavadores – in Funchal (► 42–43). Elsewhere the markets are much smaller and are usually closed by lunchtime – for the best choice you need to arrive before 9.30. Markets are usually divided into two areas, with fish being sold from great white marble slabs in one half, and fruits and vegetables artfully displayed in the other half. Meat and delicatessen goods are sold from enclosed shops around the market perimeter.

Markets can be found in all the main towns from 8am to 1pm Monday to Friday. The following are some of the best:

Calheta: on seafront road.

Câmara de Lobos: on the road that skirts the western side of the harbour.

Curral das Freiras: a general market is held in the main street on Sunday mornings where a wide range of clothing and household goods, as well as edible produce, is sold.

Machico: on the eastern side of the fortress that houses the Tourist Office on the seafront road.

Ribeira Brava: next to bus station, on seafront road.

Santa Cruz: to the west of the Palm Beach lido on the seafront esplanade.

SHOPPING CENTRES
Dolce Vita Shopping Centre
Large new multistorey shopping complex just off the main avenue, near the Infante roundabout.

✉ Rua da Ribeira de São João ⏰ Daily 10–10

Casa do Turista
The Casa do Turista offers a comprehensive selection of Madeiran and Portuguese products under one roof. The shop occupies an elegant townhouse in the centre of Funchal, and products such as lace, embroidery and other textiles, pottery, glass and furniture are displayed beneath ornate plastered ceilings, and fine paintings are displayed on the walls. You can browse for anything from a wicker cache pot to a complete dinner service.

✉ Rua do Conselheiro José Silvestre Ribeiro 2 ☎ 291 224 907 ⏰ Mon–Fri 10–7, Sat 10–1

Forum Madeira
The huge Forum Madeira shopping centre, at the far end of the Hotel Zone, is served by special buses whose indicator board says 'Forum Madeira'. Here you will find 86 shops, numerous cafés and a six-screen cinema. As well as a huge Pingo Doce supermarket, there are no fewer than four branches of Zara (men's, women's and children's clothing and home décor), plus shops selling shoes, bags, spots clothing, books, CDs, jewellery and accessories.

✉ Estrada Monumental 390 ⏰ Daily 10–10

Lido and Eden Mar Shopping Centre
Situated right in the heart of the Hotel Zone, this modern shopping centre includes a supermarket, clothing shops, banks, art gallery and wine shops.

✉ Rua do Gorgulho ⏰ Daily 10–7

Madeira Shopping
Similar in scale to Forum Madeira, but located further out of Funchal in the suburb of São Martinho (northwest of the city), Madeira Shopping is also served by special buses, with 100 shops, restaurants, bowling alley and cinema.

✉ São Martinho ✉ Daily 10–10 or later

Marina Shopping Centre
Three floors of shops, from electrical goods and clothing to beachwear and disco gear. Julber (Shop 238) has a good stock of maps, guides and holiday reading.

✉ Avenida Arriaga (the end nearest the Hotel Zone) 🕐 Mon–Fri 10–7, Sat 10–1 (with some shops staying open all day Sat and Sun)

WINE AND LIQUEURS
If you are interested in Madeira's wines, you'll find a warm welcome at Funchal's timeless old wine lodges, permeated with the fragrances of wood and wine and with cobbled courtyards stacked with barrels of maturing vintage wines.

Artur de Barros e Sousa
See page 71.

Diogos Wine Shop
Not only a comprehensive stock of Madeiran and Portuguese wines, but also a Columbus Museum alongside.

✉ Avenida Arriaga 48 ☎ 291 233 357 🕐 Daily 10–7

D'Oliveiras
A traditional wine lodge with free tastings.

✉ Rua dos Ferreiros 107 ☎ 291 220 784 🕐 Mon–Fri 10–7, Sat 10–1

Madeira Wine Company
The main outlet for long-established shippers.

✉ Avenida Arriaga 26 ☎ 291 740 110 🕐 Mon–Fri 10–7, Sat 10–12

ENTERTAINMENT

CABARET
Pestana Casino Park hotel

It would be hard to better the Pestana Casino Park hotel for evening entertainment. In addition to dinner dances with live acts in the restaurant, the next-door casino offers dinner shows every night from Wednesday to Saturday. In the same complex, the Copacabana Bar has dancing to live bands and DJs every night.

✉ Rua Imperatriz Dona Amélia ☎ 291 209 100

CASINOS
Casino da Madeira

The casino in Funchal is a striking building, designed by Oscar Niemeyer, the architect who created the master plan for the futuristic Brazilian capital, Brasilia. The architect said its shape was inspired by Madeira's volcanic landscape; locals call it 'the rack of lamb'. The main gambling room has French and American roulette, Black Jack, French Bank and *chemin-de-fer* tables, and the entrance area is equipped with a range of slot machines. Entrance to the casino is restricted to those aged 18 and over, so passports are required as proof of age.

✉ Avenida do Infante ☎ 291 231 121 🕐 Sun–Thu 3pm–3am, Fri–Sat 4pm–4am

DISCOS
O Molhe

Perched on top of a fortress that once guarded Funchal's harbour, in the part where cruise ships dock, O Molhe is a bar by day (daily 3pm–midnight), but turns into Madeira's chicest club on Friday and Saturday nights (midnight–6am, entry €5) playing house, dance and rock music and offering great harbour views.

✉ Forte de Nossa Senhora da Conceição, Estrada da Pontinha
☎ 291 203 840

Vespas

Vespas has been around for decades yet still manages to be cutting edge – now with a spectacular laser show.

✉ Avenida Sa Carneiro ☎ 291 234 800 🕒 Daily midnight–6am

LIVE MUSIC
Arsénio's

The plaintive style of music known as *fado (fate)* is as popular on Madeira as it is in the back streets of Lisbon, where the style was born. Arsénio's (► 58) is a good place to go to hear the music performed live as it has a long-established reputation for the quality of the singers and guitarists it brings over from the mainland to perform.

✉ Rua de Santa Maria 169 ☎ 291 224 007 🕒 Daily noon–2am

Marcelino Pãoe Vinho

If Arsénio's is full or you want to ring the changes, try the newer Marcelino Fado House for bar snacks and wine accompanied by soulful singing and guitar-playing. It's just north of the restaurant district in the Zona Velha.

✉ Travessa da Torre 22A ☎ 291 220 216 🕒 Daily 8:30pm–4am

NIGHTCLUBS
O Fugitivo

Energetic and scantily clad dancers from England and Brazil provide the entertainment at a venue that describes itself as a 'dancing pub'.

✉ Rua Imperatriz Dona Amélia 66A ☎ 291 222 003 🕒 Shows at midnight, 1:30, 3:30am

Western Madeira

The western third of Madeira used to be the least accessible: just getting to Ribeira Brava, the starting point for exploring the west, took more than an hour from Funchal. However, in 1997 transport on the island was revolutionized with the opening of the Via Rápida expressway, so that Ribeira Brava is now only 15 minutes away. From here you can explore picturesque fishing villages, bleak moorland and mountains cloaked in dense forest.

Ribeira
Brava

The south coast is one long ribbon of vineyards and banana plantations, with steep lanes linking one hamlet to the next. By contrast, the north coast road offers some of the most dramatic scenery on the island, with the boiling ocean dashing against huge black rocks and waterfalls cascading from clifftop to sea.

BOCA DA ENCUMEADA

The Boca da Encumeada (Encumeada Pass), midway between Ribeira Brava and São Vicente, is a popular stopping-off point for round-the-island tours because of the extensive views from the lookout point at the top. Weather permitting, you can see across to São Vicente on the north coast and down the Serra de Água Valley to the south coast, though more often than not you will stand in brilliant sunshine looking down over clouds.

If the weather is fine and clear, follow the Levada do Norte (Levada of the North) westwards: look for the sign to Folhadal opposite the café and climb up to the *levada* past the keeper's house. It is worth exploring this path for 2km (1.2 miles) or so; you will find an abundance of wild flowers and excellent views south.

✛ 16H ✉ On EN 104 road, 43km (27 miles) northwest of Funchal ▮▮ Snack bar (€) alongside the viewpoint car park; for more substantial meals try the

restaurant in the Residencial (€€, ☎ 291 951 282), 2km (1.2 miles) south on the road to Serra de Água 🚌 139

CALHETA

Calheta is the main town for the southwestern coast of Madeira. Every front garden hosts a colourful display of scarlet and pink geraniums, mauve bougainvillaea and purple passion flowers. If you come here on 7th or 8th September even the streets are covered in flowers as carpets of blooms are laid out to celebrate the Feast of Our Lady of Loreto.

Like most of the island's churches, Calheta's has been rebuilt many times and looks disappointingly modern at first, but inside is a large tabernacle of ebony and silver, donated by Portugal's King Manuel I (1469–1521). The sanctuary has a fine wooden ceiling in the Moorish-influenced *mudejar* style. The sweet smell of cane syrup from the factory next door may tempt you to take a tour to watch rum and molasses being produced.

In complete contrast to the rest of Madeira, Calheta has a fine golden sand beach, two, in fact – although the sand was actually imported from Morocco.

The best church in the area is the Capela dos Reis Magos (Chapel of the Three Kings) at Lombo dos Reis (between Estreito da Calheta and Jardim do Mar, west of Calheta). Here the chapel houses a rare wooden reredos, carved in Antwerp in the 16th century with a lively scene depicting the Adoration of the Magi.

✚ 3F ✉ On south coast, 61km (38 miles) west of Funchal 🍴 Marisqueria Rocha Mar (€€), east of town, on coast road to Madalena do Mar; renowned for seafood 🚌 80, 107 ❓ Sugar mill (☎ 291 822 264) open daily during working hours, except public hols

PAÚL DA SERRA

Flat, bleak and grazed by hardy free-range cows, sheep and goats, the Paúl da Serra comes as a surprise to travellers grown used to views of jagged mountain peaks. This windswept plateau offers expansive views of moorland, its wild open landscape somewhat compromised by a forest of wind turbines, built to supply electricity to the communities of the island's northern coast. Even so, it is worth coming here to look for wild bilberries in autumn and to savour the eerie atmosphere, or to enjoy the panoramic views to be had when the plateau is not enshrouded in cloud.

✚ 6E ✉ 61km (38 miles) northwest of Funchal, either side of the EN 124

PONTA DO PARGO

Visitors are drawn to the westernmost tip of Madeira by the thought that nothing now stands between them and the east coast of America except for hundreds of miles of ocean. Standing alongside the clifftop lighthouse at Ponta do Pargo, 300m (985ft) above the sea, you can try spotting fishermen who come here to catch the *pargos* (dolphin fish, no relation to the dolphin) after which Ponta do Pargo (Dolphin Point) is named. You can also pick up the Levada Calheta–Ponta do Pargo, the water channel that runs parallel to the south coast, weaving in and out of the hills as it follows the 650m (2,130ft) contour with views south to the sea and north to the Paúl da Serra plateau. Frequent bus services pass along the nearby EN 101 road, so you can park in Ponta do Pargo, walk as far as you choose and then catch a bus back to your car.

✚ 1C ✉ 77km (48 miles) west of Funchal ᴪ Casa de Chá O Fío (€) on the headland above the lighthouse 🚌 80, 107, 142

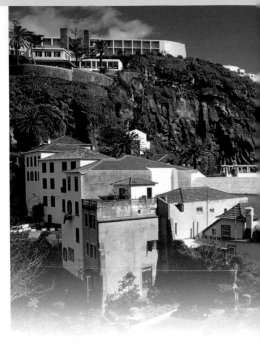

PONTA DO SOL

Sunset is a good time to visit Ponta do Sol for uninterrupted views of the western sky while strolling along the harbour promenade. Steep cobbled streets lead upwards to the church, with its unusual green ceramic font, donated by King Manuel I (1469–1521), and its ancient wooden ceilings, painted with scenes from the Life of the Virgin. Behind the church, a plaque on the wall of the new John dos Passos Cultural Centre, at Rua Príncipe D Luís I, records a visit made by John dos Passos (1896–1970), the American novelist whose grandparents emigrated from this village in the mid-19th century. The Centre has changing exhibitions and occasional dance and theatre performances.

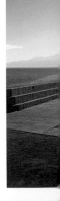

The church at nearby Madalena do Mar (sadly always locked) is the burial place of an intriguing figure known as Henrique Alemão (Henry the German) – in reality King Wladyslaw III of Poland, who chose self-imposed exile on Madeira after losing the Battle of Varna in 1414. Here he became a prosperous farmer and built a chapel on the site of today's church. Tragically, Wladyslaw drowned near Cabo Girão (▶ 38–39) as his ship hit rocks on the way to Lisbon to see King Manuel I.

✚ 13L ✉ 42km (26 miles) west of Funchal 🍴 A Poente (€) on the cliff at the eastern end of the seafront is well positioned for sunset views (☎ 291 973 579) 🚌 4, 80, 107, 115, 142, 146

PORTO DO MONIZ

Porto do Moniz is a surprisingly cosmopolitan place for a village located at the northernmost extremity of Madeira, thanks to the waterfront hotels and restaurants catering for travellers on round-the-island tours. Bones weary from walking or jolting up and down the island's roads can be revived by a good soaking in the natural rock pools of the town's bathing complex. These pools have been enlarged to create a warm sea-water bathing area, just a few feet away from the Atlantic waves that crash against Madeira's northern shore. The waves carry salt-laden spray far up into the surrounding hills, hence the ingenious use of grass and bracken fences to protect the crops growing in the fields surrounding the village. Viewed from the steep roads descending into the village, this patchwork of tiny fields and fences creates an attractive pattern.

Other attractions in Porto do Moniz include a small aquarium on the seafront and the Living Science Centre nearby, which hosts changing exhibitions.

🚻 4A ✉ 75km (47 miles) northwest of Funchal 🍴 Good choice of restaurants (€€), including the Cachalote (€€, ☎ 291 853 180), specializing in seafood 🚌 80, 139

a walk along the Levada do Risco

If you are driving across the Paúl da Serra, it is well worth breaking your journey to explore this secret valley of ancient trees and mossy waterfalls.

The turning to Rabaçal is on the north side of the ER110 as it crosses the Paúl da Serra. It is not possible to drive down the metalled road from the ER110 to Rabaçal – although there is a shuttle bus – so park in the car park alongside the main road.

Follow the winding track downhill for 2km (1.2 miles) until you come to the government rest house (with public facilities such as barbecue pits, picnic tables and toilets).

Follow the sign to the right of the rest house down the track to the Levada do Risco.

The Levada do Risco watercourse is cut into a hillside cloaked in huge gnarled tree heathers. The humid air has encouraged the growth of magnificent lichens, some resembling apple-coloured seaweed.

After five minutes' walking, a path leads left, signposted Levada das 25 Fontes (the Levada of the 25 Springs). Ignore this for now and carry straight on.

After another ten minutes' easy walking you will come to the Risco waterfall, pouring down from the rocky heights into a magical fern-hung bowl. To your left there are sweeping views down into the green valley of the River Janela, which this waterfall feeds.

Return the way you came. You can extend your walk by taking the slightly more difficult Levada das 25 Fontes, following the signposted path downhill and then turning right once you reach the levada. This will take you, after a 20-minute walk, to another fine waterfall with one main cascade and many smaller ones.

Distance 7km (4 miles)
Time 2–3 hours
Start/end point Rabaçal turning, on the ER110 ✚ 5E
Lunch No cafés in the area; take a picnic

RIBEIRA BRAVA

To understand why Ribeira Brava (Wild River) is so named, you have to visit in late autumn or winter, when the river that runs through the town centre is in full spate. For the rest of the year its harmless appearance belies its true nature. Over several thousand millennia this river has carved out a deep cleft that seems almost to divide Madeira in two, running due north from Ribeira Brava up to the Encumeada Pass and on to São Vicente, on the north coast of Madeira. The road that runs up this valley has long been an important transport route, which is why Ribeira Brava has grown into a sizeable town, with a market and a number of seafront cafés where farmers, taking their produce to Funchal, stop to break their journey.

Just back from the seafront is the splendid Church of São Bento (St Benedict). Like most churches on Madeira it has been rebuilt many times, but there are several features remaining from the original 15th-century church, including the painted font, decorated with grapes, pomegranates and wild beasts, and the carved stone pulpit. The right-hand chapel contains a fine Flemish painting of the Nativity, surrounded by gilded woodwork. At the north end of town, the new Museu Etnográfico da Madeira (Madeira Ethnographic Museum) offers displays on fishing, agriculture, weaving and winemaking.

✚ 14L ✉ 32km (20 miles) west of Funchal 🍴 Good choice of cafés and restaurants (€–€€) along the seafront road, and along the cobbled main street, Rua do Visconde 🚌 7

ℹ Tourist office (☎ 291 951 675), in the Forte de São Bento, along the seafront road

Museu Etnográfico da Madeira

✉ Rua de São Francisco 24 ☎ 291 952 598 🕐 Tue–Sun 10–12:30, 2–6

along the north coast

a drive

Much of the excitement of driving along the corniche that links Porto do Moniz (► 125) and São Vicente has been dimished now that a new road has been built, enclosed within tunnels for much of its length.

However, you can still drive parts of the old road, provided you travel in a westerly direction (it is now strictly a one-way road). Badly maintained as it is, you can still enjoy one of Europe's most spectacular roads, built on a narrow shelf cut into the cliff face high above the raging sea (drive slowly and with great care).

You will want to slow down, in any event, in order to take in the spectacular coastal views. At several points, waterfalls will come cascading down on top of your car – frightening as the noise can be, Madeirans look on the positive side: 'It's a free car wash', they say.

Halfway along the route you will find the village of Seixal (► 134), worth a stop to stretch your legs and enjoy the views of vineyards clinging to the slopes behind the village. The grapes grown here go to produce the rich dry Seixal variety of Madeira wine. West of the village, a side road leads down to rock pools and concrete terraces designed for swimming.

Distance 18km (11 miles)
Time 45 minutes
Start point São Vicente ✚ 7C
End point Porto do Moniz ✚ 4A
Lunch O Virgilio (€€) ✉ On the seafront at São Vicente
☎ 291 842 467

SÃO VICENTE

São Vicente is a prosperous agricultural town, with hotels and cafés catering to travellers exploring Madeira's northern coast. The historic core has traffic-free cobbled streets lined with shops to tempt visitors, tubs brimming with flowers and houses painted a dazzling white under orange roof tiles. In the 17th-century baroque church, the painted ceiling shows St Vincent blessing the town, and the same saint appears on the elaborately carved and gilded altar, blessing a ship.

About 1.25km (0.75 mile) south of São Vicente, on the road to Lameiros, you will find the entrance to the Grutas de São Vicente (► 62).

A short, worthwhile walk along the Levada da Fajã do Rodrigues can be found about 3.5km (2 miles) south along the road to Serra

de Água. Take the second of two right turns signposted to Ginjas, and take the next left (signposted Parque Empresarial de São Vicente). After 2km (1.2 miles), take a left (signposted Miradouro) and continue for 0.5km (quarter mile) until you come to the Parque. Take the uppermost of the park roads and look for the concreted path that leads up to a forest post and picnic area. The walk starts 100m (330ft) above the picnic area, reached by a rough track that runs up to a large concrete-lined reservoir on the right. Turn right to follow the *levada* for 1km (half mile) through orchards and eucalyptus woods to reach a spectacular *caldeirão* (meaning cauldron), watered by multiple cascades.

🚌 7C ✉ 55km (34 miles) north of Funchal 🍴 Good choice of cafés and restaurants (€–€€), including the O Virgilio restaurant (€€) on the seafront (☎ 291 842 467) 🚍 6, 132, 139

SEIXAL

Seixal, midway between Porto do Moniz and São Vicente, is a good spot at which to break your journey along the north coast road (► 130). Here you can explore the rocky foreshore (follow the signs to Piscina for a group of big, sheltered rock pools) and walk out along the jetty for views of the coastal cliffs and waterfalls which rise up on either side of the tiny village, really little more than a hamlet. Excellent wine is produced locally from grapes grown in tiny vineyards clinging to the cliffs and protected from the wind and salt spray by fences constructed from dried bracken and tree heather. Grapes grown here are used in the driest of the four main types of Madeira wine.

✚ 6B ✉ 61km (38 miles) northwest of Funchal 🍴 Local wine and snacks at bar of Estalagem Brisamar guest house (€€, ☎ 291 854 476) 🚌 139

HOTELS

Estalagem da Ponta do Sol

Connoisseurs of sophisticated design will love this boutique hotel cleverly slotted onto a vertiginous cliff on the eastern side of Ponta do Sol, with a glass-walled restaurant ensuring uninterrupted ocean views, a cosy terrace bar and rooms with similar views reached by a series of bridges and towers.

✉ Quinta da Rochinha, Ponta do Sol ☎ 291 970 200; www.pontadosol.com

Jardim do Atlântico (€€€)

See page 76.

Residencial Orca (€€)

This small 12-room hotel is perched above the rock pools at Porto do Moniz on the northwestern-most tip of Madeira. Though there are newer hotels in the village, no other allows you to fall asleep to the sound of the waves, and the restaurant serves a good selection of fresh fish dishes.

✉ Sitio das Poças, Porto do Moniz ☎ 291 850 000

RESTAURANTS

Borda d'Água (€)

With a terrace for fair-weather dining and a glassed-in dining room for when the sea spray gets too rough, this inexpensive restaurant serves standard Madeiran fare.

✉ Ribeira Brava, on the seafront (western end) ☎ No phone 🕐 Lunch, dinner 🚌 4, 6, 7, 80, 107, 115, 127, 139, 142, 146

Cachalote (€€)

Enjoy fine views of the waves breaking against the rocky foreshore of Madeira's northern coast. The locally caught fish and seafood served here is as fresh as it can be.

✉ Porto do Moniz, on the seafront ☎ 291 853 180 🕐 Lunch, dinner 🚌 8, 139

Ferro Velho (€)

This pub, serving hearty fish and meat dishes, is great value; decorative ironwork (the name means 'old iron') dots the garden while the interior is home to a collection of football club scarves.

✉ Rua da Fonte Velha ☎ 291 842 763 🕐 Lunch, dinner 🚌 Bus 6, 132, 139

Marisqueiria Rocha Mar (€€)

The best in town for fresh fish and seafood, with tables on a raised terrace looking across to the luxury yachts moored in the marina.

✉ Vilhaha Calheta ☎ 291 823 600 🕐 Lunch, dinner 🚌 80, 107, 142

Olhos d'Agua (€)

A seafront café with outdoor tables overlooking the rocks of Porto do Moniz, serving excellent *doces* (portions), *tapas*-like plates of octopus casserole, swordfish roe, limpets and grilled prawns, as well as the more usual grilled steaks, fish, omelettes and salads.

✉ Esplanada do Porto do Moniz ☎ No phone 🕐 Lunch, dinner 🚌 8, 139

Orca (€€)

The fact that many tour parties stop off here for lunch on their round-the-island tours should not be taken as a sign that the food is inferior fare. On the contrary, everything is fresh and well presented and the portions are large. Good views over the rock pools of Porto Moniz.

✉ Porto do Moniz, on south side of main square ☎ 291 850 000 🕐 Lunch, dinner 🚌 8, 139

Polo Norte (€)

The North Pole has a snack bar as well as a formal dining room, and is therefore a good choice if you just want a light meal or your children are hungry for a burger.

✉ Porto do Moniz, on north side of main square ☎ 291 853 322 🕐 Lunch, dinner 🚌 8, 139

Central Madeira

Central Madeira combines both the suburban sprawl of Funchal and the cinder-strewn volcanic landscape of the island's central mountain range. Though they are only 30 minutes' drive apart, one is rarely visible from the other since more often than not cloud obscures the mountain peaks.

Santana

The mountains are easy enough to reach, thanks to the road that goes to the top of Pico do Arieiro, Madeira's third highest peak. Once there, paths invite exploration of the endless series of knife-edge ridges that extend to the horizon in every direction. Beyond the central mountain range, the north side of the island is dotted with tiny hamlets surrounded by a patchwork of terraced fields and orchards, plantations producing willow for basket-making, and thatched cow byres.

CABO GIRÃO

Best places to see, ➤ 38–39.

CÂMARA DE LOBOS

The much-photographed fishing village of Câmara de Lobos owes its appeal to the small fleet of fishing boats based here, brightly painted in primary colours and drawn up on the town's small pebble beach for much of the day. On the eastern side of the harbour there is a small boatyard where you can watch boats being made and repaired. Local fishermen go out at night to catch *espada* (scabbard fish), which live at depths of 800m (2,625ft) or more (hence their big eyes, needed to see in the gloom). At night they come up to feed, and that is when they are most easily caught, using long lines, each with 150 or so hooks, baited with squid.

To see the catch being brought in you need to be up early: by 7am most of the fish will have been cleaned and despatched to Funchal market. The fishermen, meanwhile, celebrate the night's catch by filling the local bars. You are likely to encounter some poverty in the village, especially in the alleys leading west from the harbour, where large families live in tiny single-roomed houses, crammed up against the cliff face. Here you will also find the simple fishermen's chapel, its walls painted with naïve scenes showing the Life of St Anthony, including a storm-tossed ship in which he sailed from Italy to Portugal, and a sermon he preached that was so eloquent even the fish gathered to listen – both appropriate subjects for a fishing village.

✚ 17M ✉ 14km (8.5 miles) west of Funchal 🍴 Good choice of cafés and restaurants (€–€€), including Churchill's (€€, ☎ 291 941 541), on the east side of the harbour 🚌 Most westbound buses go to Câmara de Lobos, including 4, 6, 107, 154

CURRAL DAS FREIRAS
Best places to see, ➤ 40–41.

FAIAL
Faial is worth a brief stop for the views to be had from the *miradouro* (viewpoint) overlooking the Ametade Valley, west of the village. In the centre of the village is the new bridge that replaced one swept away in flash floods in 1980, spanning the Ribeira Séca (Dry River), which lives up to its name most of the time but can rise to a raging torrent with the autumn rains. The *miradouro* west of the village is the best spot to take in the gaunt heights of Penha de Águia (Eagle Rock), the peak that overshadows Faial, rising sheer from the sea to a height of 590m (1,935ft).

✚ 21M ✉ 30km (18.5 miles) north of Funchal 🍴 Casa de Chá do Faial at Lombo do Baixo, on the EN 103 south of Faial; good views 🚌 53,

a walk up Pico Ruivo

Getting to the top of Madeira's highest peak does not require exceptional skills in mountaineering since there is a good paved path all the way to the summit, but you do need to carry a light jacket as it can be cold on the mountain top, and you should take adequate precautions against sunburn.

Start early for the best panoramas: by the middle of the morning warm air rising from the coastal regions will have condensed on meeting the colder air of the mountains, forming clouds that, although lending their own charm to the scene, limit the views.

To reach the path, drive from Santana (➤ 148–151) along the EN 101-5 to the car park where the road runs out at Achada do Teixeira (1,592m/5,223ft).

Near the car park is the curious rock formation known as Homem em Pé (Man on Foot), a group of eroded basalt dykes.

The well-trodden path to Pico Ruivo (Red Peak) leads west from here. After some 45 minutes, the path divides; take the path to the right up through a gate and on to the government rest house, a prominent white building. Two minutes on, the path divides and you take the left fork.

*From here it is a scramble over rough boulder steps to the Pico
Ruivo summit (1,861m/6,454ft), but the effort is well worth
while for the breathtaking views of the central mountain range,
and of the island of Porto Santo (➤ 175–186), floating in the
sea away to the northeast.*

Distance 3.5km (2 miles)
Time 2 hours
Start/end point Achada do Teixeira rest house ➕ 11D 🚍 Taxi required
Lunch O Colmo (➤ 153)

MONTE

High above Funchal, the hill town of Monte is now easily reached thanks to the new cable car that runs from the Zona Velha (▶ 54–55). A second cable car also links Monte with the Jardim Botânico (▶ 86–87).

Apart from the famous Monte toboggan ride (▶ 44–45), there are several reasons to come to Monte. One is to visit the Church of Nossa Senhora (Our Lady), whose spotlit façade is a prominent landmark at night, visible on the hillside high above Funchal. Fronting the church is a flight of 74 steps. Penitents scramble up these on their knees during the festivities for the Feast of the Assumption (15 August). Inside the church is a statue of the Virgin housed in a silver tabernacle. It is said that the 15th-century statue was given to a Madeiran shepherd girl by the Virgin herself, and it is credited with many miracles. The north chapel contains the imposing black coffin of the Emperor Charles I, who died of pneumonia on Madeira in 1922, aged 35.

At the foot of the church steps is a stretch of cobbled road marking the start of the Monte toboggan ride, and toboggan drivers hang about here, waiting for customers. The Jardim do Monte municipal garden is to the north of the steps, built around a short stretch of railway viaduct, now smothered in tropical greenery. The viaduct is a vestige of the rack-and-pinion railway that once linked Monte to Funchal. Having opened in 1894 to take tourists up and down, the railway was closed after an accident in 1939, when an engine blew up, killing four people.

In the opposite direction, it's a short walk to the **Monte Palace Tropical Garden,** laid out over 7ha (17 acres) of lush hillside. Here you can explore the garden's maze of paths leading to fishponds, grottoes and bridges, Japanese-style gates and gushing fountains. A short way back down the road to Funchal another garden has opened in the grounds of the **Quinta Jardins do Imperador,** where the Emperor Charles I lived out his brief exile.

✚ 19H ✉ 6km (4 miles) north of Funchal 🍴 Cafés (€) on main square, and café/restaurant (€€) in Monte Palace Tropical Garden and in gardens of Quinta do Monte hotel (€) 🚡 Teléfericos da Madeiras, Teléfericos de Jardim Botânico or buses 20, 21, 22 ❓ Feast of the Assumption, 15 Aug

Monte Palace Tropical Garden

✉ Caminho do Monte 174 ☎ 291 782 339 🕐 Daily 9:30–6

Quinta Jardins do Imperador

✉ Caminho do Pico ☎ 291 780 460 🕐 Daily 10–6

PICO DO ARIEIRO

Best places to see, ➤ 50–51.

PONTA DELGADA

The beachside church in Ponta Delgada contains the charred figure of the crucified Christ, which is taken in procession round the village during one of Madeira's biggest religious festivals, celebrated on the first Sunday in September. The miraculous figure was found washed up on the shore in the 16th century. In 1908 it survived a fire, which destroyed the rest of the church (now rebuilt and with a superb modern ceiling painting). Across from the church is a new swimming pool complex with café.

The neighbouring village of Boaventura stands in a humid and fertile valley where willow plantations supply the raw material for the island's wicker industry (➤ 156–157). The palm-shaded cemetery shelters the grave of Miss Turner (died 1925), who never visited the spot in her lifetime but desired to be buried here because of her gardener's vivid accounts of the area's scenic beauty.

✚ 9E ✉ 51km (32 miles) north of Funchal 🍴 Solar de Boaventura (€€, ☎ 291 860 888), in Boaventura. Organic homegrown herbs, salads and vegetables 🚌 6

RIBEIRO FRIO

Ribeiro Frio is a delightful spot set among scented woodland. Here the fresh clean waters of the Ribeiro Frio ('cold stream') are channelled into a series of deep pools to create a small trout farm. Trout inevitably feature on the menu of the restaurants nearby. Woodland glades on the opposite side of the road are planted with flowering trees and shrubs to create a miniature botanical garden, where basking butterflies add to the colour.

Ribeiro Frio is the meeting point of several *levada* walks. The easiest is the walk to Balcões, which you can pick up by walking downhill from the trout farm and taking the broad track to the left that runs alongside the *levada*. Follow the wide level path for about 20 minutes to reach Balcões, whose name means 'balcony'. The reason becomes obvious when you arrive: stunning landscapes open up from this hillside viewpoint across the sun-dappled Ametade Valley to the Penha de Águia (Eagle Rock), and as far as Porto Santo. The *levada*, but not the walk, continues for another 2km (1.2 miles), with views of the peaks around Pico do Arieiro (➤ 50–51). On the opposite side of the road is Levada do Furado, signposted to Portela. If you walk as far as the bridge over the River Bezerro (allow an hour) you will experience a sequence of splendid views across central Madeira's mountainous green interior.

🚩 20K ✉ 14km (8.5 miles) north of Funchal 🍽 Restaurante Ribeiro Frio (€€, ☎ 291 575 898), opposite the trout farm 🚌 56, 103, 138

around central Madeira

This drive takes a whole day, encompassing fishing ports and wave-battered cliffs, green valleys and volcanic peaks.

Start early and head for Câmara de Lobos (➤ 138–139), hoping to catch the last of the bustle surrounding the town's fish market. Continue to Cabo Girão (➤ 38–39) for a dizzying peep over the top of one of Europe's highest sea cliffs.

At Ribeira Brava (➤ 129) you can enjoy a reviving cup of coffee in a seafront café before exploring the Manueline Church of São Bento.

Drive north up the terraced slopes of the valley of the Ribeira Brava to Boca da Encumeada (➤ 120–121) for views of the northern and southern coast of Madeira. Descend through woodland to São Vicente (➤ 132–133) and then follow the meandering north coast eastwards.

You may want to stop and swim at Ponta Delgada (➤ 144) before continuing on to Santana (➤ 148–151) for lunch or shopping, or to explore the theme park.

If you are feeling energetic, consider climbing Pico Ruivo (➤ 140–141). Alternatively, continue to Faial (➤ 139) and drive south to Ribeiro Frio (➤ 144–145) for a gentle stroll to Balcões. A third option is to continue on to the Poiso pass and drive west to the summit of Pico do Arieiro (➤ 50–51). From the Poiso pass the road descends via Terreiro da Luta (➤ 151) to Monte (➤ 142–143), where you can explore the Monte Palace Tropical Garden (open till 6, closed Sundays) before the short drive back to Funchal.

Distance 120km (75 miles)
Time 8 hours
Start/end point Funchal ✚ 19M
Lunch O Virgílio (➤ 153)

SANTANA

Santana's predominant colours are the greens of terraced fields and hay meadows, interspersed by apple, pear and cherry

orchards. Dotted among the haystacks and the pollarded willows are triangular thatched buildings *(palheiros)*, used by local farmers as cow byres. Traditionally, people lived in these ingenious structures too. Many are neglected and decaying, but a government scheme to encourage their restoration means that several in Santana are still inhabited. With their brightly painted triangular facades and a roof that sweeps from the ridge to the ground, these highly distinctive A-framed buildings are unique to this part of the island.

They are also surprisingly spacious, as you will discover if you visit the Parque Temático da Madeira, located 1km (0.5 miles) southwest of the town centre. As well as fully furnished houses, a corn mill and craft centre, the

theme park has plenty of play areas to keep energetic children
amused and some excellent exhibits on the island's history and
culture (➤ 62).

The EN 101-5 road south leads to Achada do Teixeira, from
where you can walk to Pico Ruivo (➤ 140–141), Madeira's highest
peak. Further north a rough minor road leads to the government
rest house at Queimadas. This marks the start of one of Madeira's
finest *levada* walks, taking in spectacular ravines and primeval
forest. The ultimate goal (reached after about an hour) is the 300m-
high (985ft) waterfall that cascades into the pool at the bottom of
the fern- and moss-filled Caldeirão Verde (Green Cauldron).

✚ 12D ✉ Santana lies 42km (26 miles) north of Funchal 🍴 Several cafés
and restaurants (€–€€) in the theme park; O Colmo (➤ 153) 🚌 56, 103,
132, 138

TERREIRO DA LUTA

Terreiro da Luta consists of a massive monument to the Virgin,
illuminated at night and visible from downtown Funchal. The
monument was erected in 1927 in thanksgiving after German
submarines, seeking to end the use of the island as a supply base,
sank several ships and started shelling Funchal in 1916. The
bombardment ceased after prayers to the Virgin. The massive
chains surrounding the monument come from the anchors of the
Allied ships sunk in the harbour.

A short way west of the monument is the neo-Gothic terminus
of the Funchal to Monte railway, which closed in 1939 and has now
been converted into the Au Gourmet de Quinta bar and restaurant.
There are good views from the terrace, where you will find
Francisco Franco's fine sculpture (dating from 1914) of Madeira's
Portuguese discoverer, Captain Zarco.

✚ 19H ✉ 8km (5 miles) north of Funchal 🍴 Au Gourmet de Quinta opposite
(bar €, restaurant €€) 🚌 Buses 103, 138

HOTELS

Baia do Sol (€€)
This stylish hotel almost fills the seafront of this peaceful town that makes a good base for exploring the south coast.
✉ Rua Dr João Augusto Teixeira, Ponta do Sol ☎ 291 970 140

Cabanas de São Jorge (€€)
Guests at the Cabanas de São Jorge holiday village stay in round huts inspired by Zulu architecture. The huts are set among pine and eucalyptus trees, and there are fine views from the carefully tended gardens over the cliffs of Madeira's north coast.
✉ Beira da Quinta, São Jorge ☎ 291 576 291

Estalagem do Mar (€€)
The modern Estalagem do Mar has rooms that look out over the circular outdoor pool to the rocky foreshore. Facilities include an indoor heated pool, games room, sauna and gym.
✉ Sao Viçente ☎ 291 840 010

Pousada dos Vinháticos (€€)
See page 76.

Quinta do Alto de São João (€€)
Some rural manor-house hotels offer luxury at a price, but this one is luxurious and inexpensive. Set in delightful gardens – source of the vegetables and herbs used in the restaurant – the manor has a pool and sun terrace, a large reading room and friendly staff.
✉ Lombo de São João, 4km north of Ponta do Sol ☎ 291 974 188

RESTAURANTS

As Cabanas (€€)
This restaurant, hotel and shopping complex, set down in the countryside between São Jorge and Arco de São Jorge, has African-style circular huts for rooms and a circular dining room. Keen prices and excellent Madeiran food make this a popular stopping-off point.
✉ Cabanas ☎ 291 576 291 🕐 Lunch, dinner 🚌 103, 132, 138

Casa de Abrigo (€€)

Sitting in woodland in the middle of the countryside, this roadside restaurant draws its trade from hungry walkers exploring the mountainous interior of the island, and from travellers passing between the north and south of the island. The welcoming old-fashioned interior is warmed by a wood fire (at this altitude the air has a chill even in summer) which is also used for cooking the traditional Madeiran meat-on-a-spit.

✉ Poiso, at the crossroads ☎ 291 782 269 🕓 Lunch, dinner 🚌 56, 103

Eira do Serrado (€€)

Typical Madeiran food is greatly enhanced here by the stunning panoramic view of the Curral das Freiras and its surrounding wall of green cliffs.

✉ Eira do Serrado ☎ 291 710 060 🕓 Lunch, dinner 🚌 81

Encumeada Restaurant (€€)

This roadside restaurant specialises in the kind of food that you will rarely find elsewhere on the island, including the likes of rabbit, suckling pig and hearty mountain beef and vegetable casseroles.

✉ 2km (1.2 miles) south of Boca da Encumeada ☎ 291 951 282 🕓 Lunch, dinner 🚌 6, 139

O Colmo (€€)

Santana's main restaurant inevitably attracts large tour groups, but the food is excellent, ranging from pizzas and well-filled sandwiches to grilled meats and fish.

✉ Santana, main street ☎ 291 570 290 🕓 Lunch, dinner 🚌 56, 103, 132, 138

O Virgílio (€)

O Virgílio retains the atmosphere of a good village bar, serving everything from a sandwich snack to a full meal of kebabs cooked over the log fire.

✉ São Vicente, on Porto do Moniz seafront road ☎ 291 842 467 🕓 Lunch, dinner 🚌 6, 132, 139

Pico do Arieiro (€€)

This cavernous building on top of Madeira's third highest peak caters for hungry walkers with traditional Madeira fare, plus warming *poncha* (lemon juice, honey and cane spirit).

✉ Pico do Arieiro ☎ 291 230 110 🕐 Lunch, dinner

Quebra Mar (€€)

Modern seafront restaurant with panoramic ocean views thanks to its circular, glass-walled dining room, serving Maderian fare of kebabs and scabbard fish, plus grilled meats and fish.

✉ São Vicente, on the seafront ☎ 291 842 338 🕐 Lunch, dinner 🚌 6, 132, 139, 150

Quinta do Furão (€€)

The Quinta do Furão is a working wine estate where visitors are encouraged to explore the vineyards, sample locally produced wines and eat either in the snack bar or the restaurant.

✉ Achada do Gramacho, Santana ☎ 291 570 100 🕐 Lunch, dinner 🚌 103, 132, 138

Ribeiro Frio (€€)

Formerly known as 'Victor's Bar', this rustic restaurant serves fresh trout from the adjacent farm. You can have it in many different forms, from soup or smoked trout to grilled, fried and poached.

✉ Ribeiro Frio, main street ☎ 291 575 898 🕐 Lunch, dinner 🚌 103, 138

Santo Antonio (€€)

This sparkling new restaurant gives travellers the perfect excuse to stop in the hamlet of Lugar do Baixo, where once they would have blinked and driven on. On the route west from Ribeiro Brava, it's the swish glass and steel building with the wave-shaped roof right on the seafront when you enter the tunnel. Fresh fish and seafood are served with flair, and if you have children, they'll enjoy the wading birds in the lagoon alongside.

✉ Lugar do Baixo ☎ 291 972 868 🕐 Lunch, dinner 🚌 4, 80, 107, 115, 142, 146

Eastern Madeira

Although the landscapes of eastern Madeira are tamer than those of the central mountain range, they are not without their own drama, especially along the eastern spur where the island tails off in a sequence of wild cliffs and rocky islets dashed by the Atlantic waves. Inland there are lush green river valleys, some turned into manicured golf courses, others carved into tiny plots for growing fruit and vegetables.

The modern face of Madeira is represented by Santa Catarina and the free port at Caniçal, not to mention the tower blocks and holiday complexes of Madeira's second biggest town, Machico. A taste of Madeira's past survives at Caniçal, with its tuna-fishing fleet and Whaling Museum, and at Camacha, the centre of the island's wicker-weaving industry. As always on Madeira, the north coast is the place to go for solitude and a respite from modernity.

CAMACHA

The village of Camacha sits on a high plateau to the northeast of Funchal. To enjoy the panoramic views to be had from this elevated position, you have to visit the café called O Relógio (The Clock), on the main square. This former *quinta* (rural mansion) sports a squat clock tower, whose clock and bell were brought here from Liverpool in 1896 by the philanthropical Dr Michael Grabham. The eclectic and highly accomplished Grabham was an expert, among other things, on Madeiran flora, tropical fish, organs, clocks, volcanoes and electro-magnetism; once asked how he could speak with such erudition on so many subjects, he replied: 'What I do not know, I make up'.

In addition to the café and restaurant, **O Relógio** is the largest outlet on the island for Madeira's distinctive wicker products. Baskets and furniture fill every inch of available space – hanging from the ceilings as well as being piled on the floors – and nobody will pressurize you to buy as you explore the packed rooms.

Wicker is produced from the pollarded willows which thrive in the warm, humid valleys around Camacha. Cut back to a stunted and knobbly trunk each winter, the willows put out whip-like shoots, called osiers, up to 3m (10ft) in length. The osiers are placed in tanks and soaked in water until the bark is sufficiently pliable to be peeled from the core, then delivered to the cottages of wicker-workers, who boil the canes to make them supple before weaving them into everything from simple place mats and wastepaper baskets to peacock-backed chairs or ornate birdcages.

Demonstrations can sometimes be seen in the O Relógio basement, while the middle floor has a display of Noah's Ark animals and a galleon made by local weavers.

✛ 21L ✉ 16km (10miles) northeast of Funchal 🚌 29, 77, 110

O Relógio

✉ Largo da Achada, Camacha 🕐 Open daily 9–6, except public hols
☎ 291 922 114 🍴 Café (€) on the ground floor of O Relógio

CANIÇAL

Caniçal was the centre of southern Europe's last whaling station until 1981, when the trade was banned by international treaty. Instrumental in the process of achieving the ban was the Society for the Protection of Marine Mammals, which helped establish the small but informative **Museu de Baleia** (Whaling Museum), now located in the offices once used by the Caniçal whaling company. Videos and displays in the museum explain how retired Madeiran fishermen have turned from whale-hunting to conservation, putting their knowledge of sperm whale habits and migration patterns at the disposal of marine biologists who have established a marine mammal sanctuary around Madeira.

To the east of the museum is a brand new fishing port and working boatyard where fishing boats big and small, traditional and modern, are maintained and repaired. On the opposite side of the bay is Caniçal's new bathing complex and seafront restaurant.

➕ 24J ✉ 32km (20 miles) east of Funchal 🍽 Cafés (€) next to museum and along the seafront 🚌 113

Museu de Baleia

✉ Largo da Lota ☎ 291 961 407 🕑 Tue–Sun 10–12, 1–6. Closed Mon 👋 Moderate

CANIÇO

Caniço is a sprawling village of two parts. The busy old town is set inland, its attractive buildings, the tree-shaded main square and 18th-century baroque church difficult to enjoy because of the traffic. Immediately south of the square, the pink-walled Quinta Splendida has a garden (open to the public during daylight hours) full of rare tropical varieties. To the south a winding road leads to a number of clifftop resort complexes, built here to take advantage of the sun and the sea views. Non-residents can pay to use the pool and sea-bathing facilities at the Roca Mar Hotel, and the clear waters here are popular with divers. A seafront promenade leads east to another pebbly bathing spot at Praia dos Reis Magos.

➕ 21M ✉ 8km (5 miles) east of Funchal Elsidro café (€€, ☎ 291 934 342) next to the church 🚌 2, 109, 110, 155

GARAJAU

Garajau is Portuguese for 'tern', and the village is named after the attractive black-headed sea birds that nest on the nearby cliffs. You may catch sight of them hovering over the limpid blue sea before plunging into the water to catch their food.

Garajau's most prominent landmark is the huge statue of Christ,

erected in 1927. Similar to the larger and more famous statues in Lisbon and Rio de Janeiro, it stands with outstretched arms on a headland 200m (656ft) above the sea. From here you can walk down a cobbled track leading to the base of the cliffs, where a concrete causeway links several boulder-strewn coves and beaches.

✚ 21M ✉ 8km (5 miles) east of Funchal
🍴 Snack Bar O Neptuno at the lower end of Garajau's main street, on the opposite side of the road to the Dom Pedro Hotel 🚌 2, 109, 110, 155

MACHICO

Machico is where Zarco first set foot on Madeira in 1420, claiming for Portugal an island that had been known to sailors for thousands of years. Among those who got to Madeira before Zarco were Robert Machin and Anne of Hereford, shipwrecked here after their storm-tossed ship was driven out into the Atlantic from the coast of Portugal. Robert and Anne died within days of each other and were buried by the rest of the crew, who later escaped by building a raft. On finding their graves some 50 years later, Zarco is said to have named the spot Machico, in Machin's honour (in fact, it is more likely that Machico is a corruption of Monchique, Zarco's home town in Portugal).

Zarco and his fellow navigator, Tristão Vaz Teixeira, were appointed governors of Madeira in 1425, with Zarco ruling the west from Funchal, and Teixeira in charge of the east, based in

Machico. It is his statue that stands in front of the town's large 15th-century parish church.

The smaller Capela dos Milagres (Chapel of the Miracles), east of the town, is reputed to be built on the site of Machin's grave. The original church was washed away by flash floods in 1803, but the beautiful Gothic crucifix from the high altar was found floating at sea and returned by an American sailor.

Machico's third church was built in 1739. It stands on the western arm of Machico's wide bay, where the triangular fortress, built in 1706, now serves as the tourist office. This toy-town fort is partnered by the brand new cultural centre called Fórum Machico, housing a library, cinema and theatre, plus a first-floor café with sweeping views over the town's wide bay.

✛ 23K ✉ 24km (15 miles) northeast of Funchal ⏹ Cafés and restaurants in Rua do Mercado (Market Street), including Mercado Velho (► 174)
🚌 20, 23, 53, 78, 113, 156 ❓ Festa di Santissimo Sacramento (Feast of the Holy Sacrament), celebrated on the last weekend in Aug; procession in honour of Nosso Senhora de Milagres (Our Lord of Miracles) 8–9 October
ℹ Forte de Nossa Senhora do Amparo (☎ 291 962 289 ⏰ Mon–Fri 9–12:30, 2–5, Sat 9:30–12)

to Ponta de São Lourenço

Follow this switchback path to the easternmost tip of Madeira and you will feel as if you are standing on the edge of the world.

To reach the start of the walk, drive east along the EN 101-3 around Caniçal (➤ 158–159) and past Prainha beach (➤ 165), until you come to a small roundabout. The left turn leads to a well-placed miradouro with panoramic views. Take the right turn and continue to the car park at the end of the tarmac road. The path starts by the big boulders at the eastern end of the car park. So many people use the path it is well worn and impossible to miss.

To your right is the great rocky sweep of the Baía de Abra (Abra Bay), with its towering orange and brown cliffs. Beyond the bay is Ilhéu de Fora, with its lighthouse, and an eyelet in the rock called Ponta do Furado. Further out to sea are the flat-topped Ilhas Desertas, inhabited only by seabirds and a small colony of protected monk seals.

After 20 minutes or so, the uphill track meets a boulder wall, with a gap for walkers to pass through. Bear left on a rocky path and descend to the valley where the path splits.

Go left to reach a viewpoint high above three purple rocks known as the 'seahorses', with a stunning westwards view of high cliffs and raging seas.

Brave souls with a good head for heights can continue from here along the waymarked path for another 1.5km (1 mile) to the little quay called the Cais do Sardinha, a now deserted harbour named after its former owners, but for most visitors the first viewpoint will be excitement enough.

Distance 2km (1.2 miles)
Time 1.5 hours
Start/end point Car park at easternmost end of EN 101-3 road, beyond Caniçal ✚ 23G (inset)
Lunch No café nearby but stallholders occasionally turn up in the car park to sell fruit and cold drinks

PALHEIRO, JARDIMS DO

Best places to see, ➤ 48–49.

PORTO DA CRUZ

Porto da Cruz was once an important harbour town on the north coast of Madeira, thriving in an era when goods were transported from place to place by boat, but declining into a quiet backwater once road transport took over. Today it is a town in transition, its old fishing quarter, threaded by cobbled alleys, partly restored and partly still crumbling.

The old port is reached by following the road that skirts the small fortress-crowned hill to the east. Continuing round the hill, you will reach the sugar mill and distillery of the Companhia dos Enghenos do Norte. The mill stands unused for much of the year, but a sweet scent fills the air during the sugar harvesting – March to May – when production of *aguardente*, a rum-like spirit, is under way.

Something of the gloom that visitors to Porto da Cruz claim to experience is due to the shadows cast by Penha de Águia (Eagle Rock), rising to a height of 590m (1,935ft) to the west of the village. The road to the east of the village gives out at Lorano, and from here there are splendid views to be had from the clifftop path.

✚ 21H ✉ 30km (18 miles) northeast of Funchal
🍴 Praça do Engeno restaurant (€€),
Rua da Praia 🚌 53, 56, 78, 103, 138

PRAINHA

Prainha enjoys the unique distinction of having the largest natural sand beach on Madeira. Hidden from the road, the beach is reached from the car park on the road from Caniçal to Ponta de São Lourenço.

The size of the car park indicates how busy the beach can become in summer. The brown-black sand on the beach derives from the local rock, a curious mixture of crushed shell and volcanic debris, pulverized by tens of thousands of years of wave action. The sheltered, south-facing beach enjoys good views of the easternmost tip of Madeira, as well as of aeroplanes flying into nearby Santa Catarina airport.

🕂 22G (inset) ✉ 30km (18 miles) east of Funchal 🍴 Bar (€), overlooking the beach 🚌 113

around eastern Madeira

Allow at least half a day for this leisurely drive around Madeira's eastern spur, including time to swim off one of the island's few naturally sandy beaches.

Leave Funchal on the ER 101, following signs to the airport, then turn left, after 3km (2 miles), on to the ER 102 signposted to Camacha.

After 2km (1.2 miles) turn right to visit the Blandy wine-merchant family's splendid Palheiro Gardens (➤ 48–49).

Rejoin the ER 102 and continue north to Camacha (➤ 156–157). Continue along the ER 102 for a further 11km (7 miles) to Santo António da Serra.

At Santo António da Serra take a stroll in the park surrounding the Quinta da Serra (➤ 171), the home of the Blandy family before they acquired the Quinta do Palheiro Ferreiro.

Continue along the ER 101, but turn left, before reaching Machico, on the ER 101-3 signposted to Caniçal. Skirt Caniçal and continue to the end of the road for a walk out across the cliff tops at Ponta de São Lourenço (➤ 162–163).

Cool off from your walk by taking a dip in the sea at Prainha beach (➤ 165) on the way back to Caniçal, with its Whaling Museum (➤ 158). Stop at Machico (➤ 160–161), Madeira's second town, to walk around the bay and visit the three historic churches.

*Follow the coastal road beneath the airport runway to
Santa Cruz (➤ 168–169).*

Depending on the time of day, your last stop before
returning to Funchal could be Garajau (➤ 160), where you
can watch the sun go down from the clifftop alongside the
outsize statue of Christ.

Distance 60km (37 miles)
Time 6 hours
Start/end point Funchal ✉ 19M
Lunch Café O Relógio (€€) ✉ Largo da Achada, Camacha
☎ 291 922 114

SANTA CRUZ

The people of Santa Cruz get an intimate view of aeroplanes
coming into land at nearby Santa Catarina airport, which opened
in 1964, but the town manages to retain the peaceful atmosphere
of a bygone era. The parish church of 1479 is one of the oldest
on the island and echoes of Funchal's cathedral suggest that the

same architect – Pedro Enes – could have been involved in the design. Three blocks east of the main square, in Rua da Ponta Nova, is the elegant 19th-century Tribunal (Law Court), with its splendid colonial verandas and stone stairway. Flowering trees fill the park surrounding the court, while date palms and dragon trees line the seafront road, two blocks south, lending the pebble beach the air of an upmarket Riviera.

Strung out along the promenade are cafés, the village market, the Municipal Library with a small art gallery and an open-air theatre, plus the Palm Beach lido, with paddling pools, a swimming pool and sea-bathing facilities.

A more up-to-date water park – the Aquaparque (➤ 62) – is located at the other (western) end of the town. With slides, tubes and flumes, this is a great place for children to let off steam.

✚ 23K ✉ 17km (10.5 miles) east of Funchal 🍴 Cafés along the seafront (€) serving home-made cakes 🚌 20, 23, 53, 113, 128, 156

SANTO ANTÓNIO DA SERRA

The wooded slopes around Santo António da Serra (known locally as just Santo da Serra) are dotted with the elegant old mansions of the English merchants who once dominated the Madeira wine trade. Privacy, and a welcome climate several degrees cooler than downtown Funchal, made this a favoured summer retreat.

One splendid mansion, the Quinta da Serra, stands at the centre of a large public park, just off the main square, where there are a few animal enclosures and a playground. The park is at its most colourful during the spring and early summer when the first flush of camellias is superseded by the bright blooms of azaleas. Avenues running through the park lead to a viewpoint that looks out to the easternmost tip of the island.

✚ 22J ✉ 22km (13.5 miles) northeast of Funchal 🍽 Café (€) on the main square 🚌 Buses 20, 77, 78 ❓ Park open daily during daylight hours

HOTELS

Costa Linda Hotel (€)

Between the church and the sea in Costa da Cruz, this quiet hideaway has 12 simply furnished rooms, at reasonable prices, and is well located for exploring the northern coast, with Santana and the airport a short distance away thanks to new road tunnels.

✉ Porto da Cruz ☎ 291 560 080; www.costa-linda.net

Estalagem Relógio (€)

Good accommodation in the 'wicker' village of Camacha, with spectacular views from some rooms. The nearby restaurant has regular Madeiran song and dance shows by one of the island's best troupes.

✉ Sítio da Igreja, Camacha ☎ 291 922 777

Estalagem Serra Golf (€€)

The name says it all – the Estalagem Serra Golf is a short drive away from both of Madeira's golf courses and is popular with people who come to the island to play. Set among woodland, with manicured grounds and a new indoor swimming pool, the hotel has modern rooms built around the core of a 200-year-old mansion.

✉ Santo António da Serra ☎ 291 550 500; www.serragolf.com

Quinta Splendida (€€€)

See page 76.

Roca Mar (€€€)

See page 77.

Royal Orchid (€€)

This aparthotel complex, alongside the Roca Mar, has modern facilities, including indoor and outdoor pools, a Jacuzzi, a Turkish steam room and sauna, gym and games rooms. The apartments are built in terraced blocks with sea views; each studio has its own fully equipped kitchenette.

✉ Caniço de Baixo ☎ 291 934 600; www.hotelroyalorchid.com

RESTAURANTS

A Brisa do Mar (€)
Smart glass-fronted café overlooking the new lido in Caniçal
serving *doses* (dishes) of shrimps with garlic or stewed octopus
in the café, or more substantial fresh fish and skewered meats in
the restaurant.
✉ Piscinas do Caniçal ☎ 291 960 726 🕐 Lunch, dinner 🚌 113

Casa Velha do Palheiro (€€€)
Outside of Funchal's five-star hotels, it is unusual to find cooking of
such a high standard on Madeira. This elegant restaurant, in a
converted mansion on the edge of the Quinta do Palheiro estate,
serves stylish dishes which combine the best of Madeira's fresh
ingredients with ideas borrowed from Italy, the Mediterranean and
the Far East.
✉ Estalagem Casa Velha do Palheiro ☎ 291 790 350 🕐 Lunch, dinner.
Reservations advised 🚌 36, 37, 77

Fórum Machico (€)
This seafront restaurant looks stylishly expensive, with its black
walls and polished steel bar, but the menu is simple and
inexpensive: plenty of pasta choices and salads, plus fresh fish,
which you can eat on the terrace to the sound of splashing
fountains and breaking waves.
✉ Praia da Machico ☎ 291 964 009 🕐 Lunch, dinner 🚌 20, 23, 53, 78,
113, 156

Gallery Inn and Art (€€)
This friendly clifftop establishment in Caniço de Baixa combines
a restaurant, wine bar, café and hotel with a gallery of original
paintings by contemporary artists from all over the world, many
of which are for sale. Also a good range of wines.
✉ Rua da Robert B Powell, Caniço de Baixo ☎ 291 938 200 🕐 Lunch,
dinner 🚌 2, 109, 110, 136

Mercado Velho (€€)

Machico's Old Market makes an atmospheric base for this pleasant restaurant with its tree-shaded terrace and fountain.

✉ Rua do Mercado, Machico ☎ 291 965 926 🕔 Lunch, dinner 🚌 20, 23, 53, 78, 113, 156

Miradouro da Portela (€)

Several major footpaths meet at the Portela pass, and hungry hikers make up a good portion of the customers at this thatched country inn, serving huge and inexpensive portions of beef kebab cooked over a real wood fire, plus lighter soups and snacks.

✉ Portela crossroads ☎ 291 966 169 🕔 Daily 10–10 🚌 Bus 53

Pastelaria Galã (€)

Pop in here for a mid-morning snack or afternoon tea and sample the delights of Madeiran cakes, made with eggs, almonds, fruits and nuts. The small restaurant also serves snacks and sandwiches.

✉ Rua do Mercado, Machico ☎ 291 965 720 🕔 Lunch, dinner 🚌 20, 23, 53, 78, 113, 156

La Perla Gourmet Restaurant (€€€)

Set in beautifully gardened grounds, La Perla occupies a typical Madeiran *quinta*, a manor house once at the centre of a wine estate, now converted to provide a stylish restaurant. The Italian-influenced menu includes wild mushroom dishes, veal and *zabaglione*, as well as grilled fish and, in tribute to Madeira's volcanic origins, beef served sizzling on a heated volcanic stone.

✉ Quinta Splendida, Sítio da Vargem, Caniço ☎ 291 930 400 🕔 Lunch, dinner 🚌 2, 109, 110, 136

Tourigalo (€)

A family favourite located opposite the Dom Pedro hotel on Garajau's main street and serving barbecue chicken, steaks, pork and king-sized prawns – something for everyone.

✉ Garajau 142 ☎ No phone 🕔 Lunch, dinner 🚌 2, 109, 110, 136, 155

Porto Santo

Vila Baleira

Porto Santo is all about sun, sea and sand, and almost nothing else. The sleepy island is virtually flat, and there is little agriculture since Porto Santo lacks Madeira's abundant supplies of water. The island's population of 5,000 earns much of its living during July and August, when a steady stream of visitors arrives to soak up the sun and dance the night away in hotel discos.

Some take the relatively expensive 15-minute flight from Madeira, while others take a more leisurely sea journey on the Porto Santo Line's luxurious cruiser, which takes 2 hours and 40 minutes to cross the 37km (23 miles) of choppy ocean separating the two islands. Plans are afoot to develop Porto Santo's tourism further, but for now its chief attraction is that its magnificent sweep of beach remains clean, unspoiled and undeveloped.

FONTE DA AREIA

The little rain that Porto Santo receives rapidly filters through the island's sandy soils to emerge as a series of springs when the water meets impermeable basalt. The Fonte da Areia (Spring in the Sand) is one such spring, and its popularity is guaranteed by the belief that drinking its waters restores body and soul and bestows longevity. For those who prefer alternative restoratives, there is a bar alongside the public drinking fountain, with palm-shaded tables creating a tropical illusion. The spring itself fills a series of troughs that were once used by local women for washing their laundry. The nearby cliffs of compressed sand have been eroded into bizarre sculptures by wind and rain, and there are rock pools to explore on the pebbly beach below. The spring can be reached on foot by taking the road west from Camacha; the Fonte da Areia makes a good destination for a day trip and, perhaps, a picnic.

➕ *Porto Santo 4b* ✉ 3km (2 miles) northwest of Vila Baleira 🍴 Café (€) alongside the spring

PONTA DA CALHETA

This southernmost tip of Porto Santo marks the watershed between the long sweep of sandy beach running along the southern coast of the island and the rocky northern coast. A good time to come here is dusk, when the setting sun casts shadows and colours over the much-eroded rocks on the offshore islands, allowing you to exercise your imagination and see all sorts of shapes. The evening can be extended by taking a meal of fresh fish in the nearby restaurant, then walking back along the sandy beach while imagining you are in your own private paradise.

✚ *Porto Santo 3e* ✉ 5km (3 miles) southwest of Vila Baleira 🍴 O Calhetas restaurant (€€, ☎ 291 984 380) at the point where the coastal road ends

PORTELA

The *miradouro* (viewpoint) at Portela may not be the highest point on Porto Santo, but it is the best place to get a sense of the scale of the pure sandy beach that seems to stretch endlessly along the southern coast. It will also give you an idea of why Porto Santo is known as the 'tawny island'. Deforestation at a very early stage in the island's history led to rapid erosion of the fertile topsoil, leaving the sand-coloured landscape you see today.

✚ *Porto Santo 6c* ✉ 1.5km (1 mile) northeast of Vila Baleira

SERRA DO DENTRO

The landscape of the Serra do Dentro valley, forming the eastern part of the island, looks like the setting for a Wild West movie with its arid sheep- and cattle-grazed slopes. The terraces, abandoned farmhouses and threshing floors are all that remain of communities that gave up the struggle to scratch a living from the thin soil, while reservoirs and stunted tree saplings indicate government schemes to restore life to the area.

 *Porto Santo 6b* ✉ 5km (3 miles) northeast of Vila Baleira

a walk

through the quarries and coves of Porto Santo

Geological formations and beautiful coves are found at the unspoiled southwestern tip of Porto Santo. Heading for Calheta by bus, taxi, car or bicycle, you pass the turning for Campo de Baixo, with its church of Esprito Santo (Holy Spirit) and look for the next turn right. If you come by car you can park here.

Walk up the track, turning left after 50m (55yds), and continue to the little white chapel of São Pedro (St Peter), originally built in the 17th century.

As you continue straight on, climbing the low conical hill called the Pico de Ana Ferreira (283m/928ft), you will reach a redundant quarry remarkable for its much-photographed basalt columns, popularly known as 'organ pipes', that are formed by the slow cooling of volcanic magma.

Return the way you came to the main coast road and continue towards Calheta. After 2.5km (1.5 miles), take another right turn and after 0.75km (0.4 miles) look for a path on the left that climbs then descends for 0.75km (0.4 miles).

At the end of the descent you will reach the tiny beach and clear turquoise waters of the cove at Zimbralinho (shaded from mid afternoon, so aim to get here by the middle of the day if you want the best sunshine).

Retracing your steps, continue west until the road runs out at Ponta da Calheta.

The café here is a good spot to enjoy a long lazy lunch with views that, on a clear day, stretch to Madeira. Afterwards you can swim before taking the bus back to Vila Baleira (last departure 6.20pm).

Distance 5.5km (3.5 miles) on foot
Time 3 hours
Start point Vila Baleira ✚ *Porto Santo 5c*
End point Ponta da Calheta ✚ *Porto Santo 3e*
Lunch O Calhetas (➤ 186)

VILA BALEIRA

Vila Baleira is Porto Santo's capital, and it is here that most of the island's 5,000 inhabitants live. The town was founded by Bartolomeu Perestrelo, the first governor, who did not draw the short straw you might think from the island's present appearance: in the 15th century it was a profitable colony, producing cereals, wines and sugar, as well as dyestuffs from the sap of dragon trees.

Two dragon trees survive in the town's main square, Largo do Pelourinho, flanking the entrance to the 16th-century Town Hall, with its handsome double staircase and 16th-century stone doorframe. Alongside is the popular Bar Gel Burger, the centre of the island's social life. To the north is the much-restored parish church, with only a small side chapel surviving from the 15th-century Gothic original. From opposite the Town Hall, Rua Infante D Henrique, the town's palm-lined main street, leads straight to tho beach, the objective of most visitors.

In the street behind the church is the **Casa Museu Cristóvão Colombo,** reputed to be the house in which Christopher Columbus lived during his stay on Porto Santo. There is a good library of books in English, Portuguese and other languages, from which you can learn all there is to know about the famous Genoese explorer, and several imaginative portraits and amusing prints depict the arrival of some of the first Europeans to land on American shores.

➕ *Porto Santo 5c* ✉ On the southern coast of Porto Santo, 10 minutes' drive from the airport 🍴 The Baiana café (€, ☎ 291 984 649), on Largo do Pelourinho, serves excellent grilled fish

ℹ️ Rua Dr Henrique Vieira de Castro ☎ 982 361

Casa Museu Cristóvão Colombo

☎ 291 952 598 🕐 Tue–Fri 10–12:30, 2–5:30, Sat 10–1 (Jul–Sep only). Closed Sun, public hols

a drive around Porto Santo

Take a taxi, or rent a car, for a half-day tour of Porto Santo's main sights.

From Vila Baleira follow Rua Bispo D E de Alencastre eastwards (signposted to Serra de Fora).

The road takes you to the viewpoint at Portela (➤ 178) and on to the farming villages of Serra de Fora and Serra do Dentro (➤ 179). The views change as you swing round the north side of the island to Camacha, with its restored windmill and the Estrela do Norte restaurant (➤ 186), which is housed in an old farmhouse and specializes in barbecued chicken.

In Camacha, take the minor road that leads to the Fonte da Areia to sample the waters, which are reputed to bestow eternal youth on those who drink them. Return to the main road and drive south for 2km (1 mile), then turn left on the minor road that goes to the viewpoint on Pico do Castelo (437m/1,434ft).

From the cone-shaped peak there are sweeping views over the whole island, with the airport runway prominent in the plain to the west. On the summit you will find the scant remains of the fortification after which the Pico do Castelo is named. Islanders used to take refuge on those frequent occasions when pirates raided Vila Baleira. Warning bonfires were lit on the neighbouring hill, called Pico do Facho (Beacon Peak), the island's highest point at 517m (1,696ft).

You can walk from one peak to the other through pine plantations before heading back downhill for the short return stretch to Vila Baleira.

Distance 15km (10 miles)
Time 3 hours
Start/end point Vila Baleira ✛ *Porto Santo 5c*
Lunch Estrela do Norte (➤ 186)

HOTELS

Luamar (€€)
Right among the sand dunes of Port Santo's beach; rooms have kitchenettes. A shuttle bus runs to Vila Baleira.
✉ Sítio de Cabeço de Ponta ☎ 984 121 🕙 May–Oct only

Pensão Central (€)
The small and friendly Central is a short, steep walk up from the heart of Vila Baleira. What it lacks in big hotel services, it makes up for with bargain-priced, clean and comfortable rooms.
✉ Rua A M Vasconcelos ☎ 982 226

Porto Santo (€€€)
See page 76.

RESTAURANTS

Baiana (€)
The Baiana's menu features many different varieties of charcoal-grilled fish, as well as grilled chicken, steak and hearty fish stew.
✉ Rua Dr Nuno S Teixeira 9 ☎ 984 649 🕙 10am to midnight

Estrela do Norte (€)
Busy bar with an open-air terrace serving inexpensive charcoal-grilled fish and chicken.
✉ Camacha ☎ 983 500 🕙 Lunch, dinner; reservations a must in high season

O Calhetas (€€€)
Serves wonderful grilled fish, but is best known for its glorious views of the setting sun from Porto Santo's southernmost tip.
✉ Ponta da Calheta beach ☎ 984 380 🕙 Lunch, dinner

O Forno (€€)
A variation on the usual theme of *espetada* kebabs is the house speciality, *picado*, consisting of small chunks of beef spiced up with garlic and chilli.
✉ Avenida Viera de Castro, Vila Baleira ☎ 985 141 🕙 Lunch, dinner; reservations essential in high season

Sight Locator Index

This index relates to the maps on the covers. We have given map references to the main sights of interest in the book. Grid references in italics indicate sights featured on the town plan of Funchal and the map of Porto Santo. Some sights within towns may not be plotted on the maps.

Index

Acknowledgements

The Automobile Association would like to thank the following photographers, companies and picture libraries for their assistance in the preparation of this book.

Abbreviations for the picture credits are as follows – (t) top; (b) bottom; (c) centre; (l) left; (r) right; (AA) AA World Travel Library.

4l Palheiro Gardens, AA/C Sawyer; **4c** Airport, AA/P Baker; **4r** Pico do Arieiro, AA/C Sawyer; **5l** Palacio de São Lourenço, AA/P Baker; **5r** Former Monte Palace Hotel, AA/J Wyand; **6/7** Palheiro Gardens, AA/C Sawyer; **8/9** African lilies, AA/C Sawyer; **10/11t** Madeiran landscape, AA/C Sawyer; **10bl** Palheiro Gardens, AA/C Sawyer; **10br** North Coast Drive, AA/C Sawyer; **11b** Levada walking, AA/J Wyand; **12bl** Scabbard fish, AA/P Baker; **12br** Home-made bread, AA/J Wyand; **12/3t** Zona Velha, AA/C Sawyer; **13tr** Câmara de Lobos, AA/J Wyand; **13b** Mercado dos Lavradores in Funchal, AA/J Wyand; **14t** Bolo de Mel, AA/J Wyand; **14b** Produce for sale, AA/J Wyand; **14/5** Adegas de São Francisco, AA/C Sawyer; **15t** Lapas, AA/J Wyand; **15bl** Golfinho restaurant, AA/J Wyand; **15br** Local man, AA/J Wyand; **16/7** Street scene, AA/C Sawyer; **16bl** Adegas de São Francisco AA/C Sawyer; **16br** Palheiro Gardens, AA/C Sawyer; **17t** Rainbow in the mountains, AA/P Baker; **17c** Levada, AA/J Wyand; **17b** Zona Velha (Old Town) in Funchal, AA/J Wyand; **18/9** Annual flower festival, AA/C Sawyer; **19t** Curral das Freiras, AA/C Sawyer; **19bl** Boat in harbour, AA/C Sawyer; **19br** Espetada, AA/P Baker; **20/1** Airport, AA/P Baker; **24** Annual flower festival, AA/C Sawyer; **25** Wine festival, AA/J Wyand; **26** Airport, AA/P Baker; **27** Coastal road, AA/P Baker; **29** Annual summer festival, AA/J Wyand; **30** Bank, AA/J Wyand; **32** Policeman, AA/P Baker; **34/5** Pico do Arieiro, AA/C Sawyer; **36** Adegas de São Francisco, AA/C Sawyer; **36/7** Adegas de São Francisco, AA/C Sawyer; **37** Adegas de São Francisco, AA/C Sawyer; **38/9** Cabo Girão, AA/C Sawyer; **40/1** Curral das Freiras, AA/C Sawyer; **41t** Curral das Freiras, AA/C Sawyer; **42** Mercado dos Lavradores in Funchal, AA/J Wyand; **43** Mercado dos Lavradores in Funchal, AA/P Baker; **44/5** The Monte Toboggan Ride, AA/C Sawyer; **45t** Tiles depicting the Monte Toboggan Ride, AA/J Wyand; **46** Museu de Arte Sacra in Funchal, AA/J Wyand; **46/7** Museu de Arte Sacra in Funchal, AA/J Wyand; **48** Palheiro Gardens, AA/C Sawyer; **48/9** Palheiro Gardens, AA/C Sawyer; **49** Palheiro Gardens, AA/C Sawyer; **50/1** Pico do Arieiro, AA/C Sawyer; **52** Sé (Funchal Cathedral) AA/C Sawyer; **52/3** Sé (Funchal Cathedral) AA/C Sawyer; **54** Zona Velha (Old Town) in Funchal, AA/J Wyand; **54/5** Zona Velha (Old Town) in Funchal, AA/J Wyand; **56/7** Palacio de São Lourenço, AA/P Baker; **59** Café, AA/C Sawyer; **60/1** Sunset at Ponta de São Lourenço, AA/J Wyand; **62/3** Lido Complex in Funchal, AA/J Wyand; **64/5** Lizard, © blickwinkel/Alamy; **65** Hiking trail at a levada, Photolibrary Group; **66** Barrel at the Madeira Wine Company in Funchal, AA/J Wyand; **69** Adegas de São Francisco Wine Lodge, AA/J Wyand; **70** Embroidery, AA/J Wyand; **72/3** Scuba diving, Porto Santo Diving Centre; **74** Traditional dancing, AA/P Baker; **77** Reid's Palace, AA/J Wyand; **78/9** Former Monte Palace Hotel, AA/J Wyand; **81** Street scene, AA/C Sawyer; **83** Convento de Santa Clara, AA/C Sawyer; **84** Fortaleza de São Tiago, AA/C Sawyer; **84/5** IBTAM Handicrafts Institute, AA/C Sawyer; **86/7** Jardim Botânico, AA/J Wyand; **87** Jardim dos Loiros, AA/J Wyand; **88/9** Jardim de Santa Catarina, AA/C Sawyer; **90** Tiles at the Museu 'A Cidade do Açúcar, AA/J Wyand; **92/3** Museu Franco, AA/J Wyand; **94** Painting at the Museu Freitas, AA/J Wyand; **94/5** Museu Municipal, AA/J Wyand; **96** Praça do Município, AA/C Sawyer; **98** O Pátio AA/C Sawyer; **99** Funchal, AA/J Wyand; **101** Quinta das Cruzes, AA/C Sawyer; **119** North Coast Drive, AA/C Sawyer; **120/1** Boca da Encumeada, AA/C Sawyer; **121** Calheta, AA/J Wyand; **122** Ponta do Pargo, AA/J Wyand; **123** Paúl da Serra, AA/J Wyand; **124/5** Ponta do Sol, AA/C Sawyer; **125** Porto do Moniz, Roberto Pereira; **127** Levada do Risco, AA/C Sawyer; **128/9** Ribeira Brava, AA/P Baker; **131** North Coast Drive, AA/C.Sawyer; **132/3** São Vicente, AA/C Sawyer; **134** North Coast Drive, AA/C Sawyer; **137** Pico Ruivo, imagebroker/Alamy; **138/9** Câmara de Lobos, AA/J Wyand; **140/1** Pico Ruivo, AA/J Wyand; **142t** Toboggan run in Monte, AA/C Sawyer; **142/3** Monte Palace Tropical Garden, AA/C Sawyer; **144** Ponta Delgada, AA/J Wyand; **144/5** Ribeiro Frio AA/C Sawyer; **145**, Lady knitting at Ribeiro Frio, AA/C Sawyer; **147** Cabo Girão, AA/J Wyand; **148/9** Santana, AA/C Sawyer; **150** Terreiro da Luta, AA/J Wyand; **155** Beach, AA/C Sawyer; **156t** Camacha AA/P Baker; **156b** Camacha, AA/P Baker; **156/7** Wicker weavers, AA/C Sawyer; **158t** Caniçal, AA/P Baker; **158/9** Beach, AA/C Sawyer; **159** Caniço, AA/J Wyand; **160** Christo Rei statue, Photolibrary Group; **160/1** Machico, AA/C Sawyer; **162/3** Ponta de São Lourenço, AA/P Baker; **164/5** Ponta da Cruz, AA/J Wyand; **167** Machico, AA/C Sawyer **168/9** Santa Cruz, AA/P Baker; **170** Santo António da Serra, AA/P Baker; **171** Santo António da Serra, AA/P Baker; **175** Porto Santo harbour, AA/J Wyand; **176** Fonte da Areia in Porto Santo, DRTM; **176/7** Calheta in Porto Santo, Marcial Fernandes; **178/9** Porto Santo, AA/J Wyand; **181** Passeios in Porto Santo, Marcial Fernandes; **182** Porto Santo AA/J Wyand; **184** Porto Santo, AA/J Wyand.

Every effort has been made to trace the copyright holders, and we apologise in advance for any accidental errors. We would be happy to apply the corrections in the following edition of this publication.

Dear Reader

Your comments, opinions and recommendations are very important to us. Please help us to improve our travel guides by taking a few minutes to complete this simple questionnaire.

You do not need a stamp (unless posted outside the UK). If you do not want to cut this page from your guide, then photocopy it or write your answers on a plain sheet of paper.

Send to: **The Editor, AA World Travel Guides,
FREEPOST SCE 4598, Basingstoke RG21 4GY.**

Your recommendations...

We always encourage readers' recommendations for restaurants, nightlife or shopping – if your recommendation is used in the next edition of the guide, we will send you a **FREE AA Guide** of your choice from this series. Please state below the establishment name, location and your reasons for recommending it.

_____
_____
_____
_____
_____
_____

Please send me **AA Guide** _____

About this guide...
Which title did you buy?
    AA _____
Where did you buy it? _____
When? m m / y y
Why did you choose this guide? _____
_____
_____
_____
_____

Did this guide meet your expectations?

Exceeded ☐   Met all ☐   Met most ☐   Fell below ☐

Were there any aspects of this guide that you particularly liked? _____
_____
_____
_____

continued on next page...

Is there anything we could have done better? _____

_____

_____

_____

About you...

Name (Mr/Mrs/Ms) _____

Address _____

_____

_____ Postcode _____

Daytime tel nos _____

Email _____

Please only give us your mobile phone number or email if you wish to hear from us about other products and services from the AA and partners by text or mms, or email.

Which age group are you in?
Under 25 ☐   25–34 ☐   35–44 ☐   45–54 ☐   55–64 ☐   65+ ☐

How many trips do you make a year?
Less than one ☐   One ☐   Two ☐   Three or more ☐

Are you an AA member? Yes ☐   No ☐

About your trip...

When did you book? m m / y y   When did you travel? m m / y y

How long did you stay? _____

Was it for business or leisure? _____

Did you buy any other travel guides for your trip? _____

If yes, which ones? _____

_____

_____

Thank you for taking the time to complete this questionnaire. Please send it to us as soon as possible, and remember, you do not need a stamp (unless posted outside the UK).

AA Travel Insurance call 0800 072 4168 or visit www.theAA.com